Washington

WASHINGTON BY ROAD

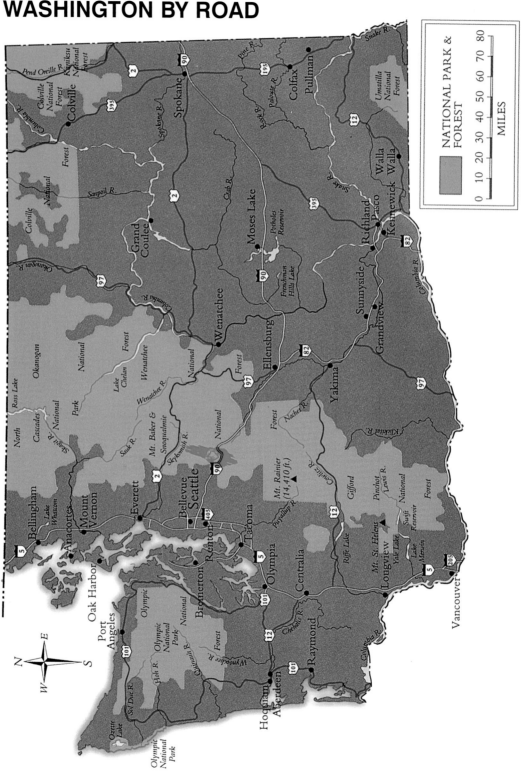

Celebrate the States

Washington

Rebecca Stefoff

mc **Marshall Cavendish**
Benchmark
New York

Marshall Cavendish Benchmark
99 White Plains Road
Tarrytown, NY 10591-9001
www.marshallcavendish.us

Library of Congress Cataloging-in-Publication Data

Stefoff, Rebecca
Washington / by Rebecca Stefoff. — 2nd ed.
p. cm. — (Celebrate the states)
Summary: "Provides comprehensive information on the geography, history, wildlife, governmental
structure, economy, cultural diversity, peoples, religion, and landmarks of Washington"
—Provided by publisher.
Includes bibliographical data and index.
ISBN-13: 978-0-7614-2561-8
1. Washington (State)—Juvenile literature. I. Title. II. Series.
F891.3.S72 2007
979.7—dc22 2006032436

Editor: Christine Florie
Publisher: Michelle Bisson
Art Director: Anahid Hamparian
Series Designer: Adam Mietlowski

Photo research by Connie Gardner

Cover photo by age fotostock/SuperStock
The photographs in this book are used by permission and through the courtesy of:
SuperStock: James Lemass, back cover; age fotostock, 105; *AP Photo:* Kevin P. Casey, 63; Ted S. Warren,
76, 78; *PhotoEdit:* Dennis MacDonald, 72; *Corbis:* Charles Mauzy, 8, 10; Joseph Sohm, 11; Kevin
Schafer, 12; Wolfgang Kaehler, 15; Craig Tuttle, 19; Wayne Lockwood, 20; Stuart Westmorland, 23,
102; George Steinmetz, 26; Museum of History and Industry, 43; Underwood and Underwood, 49;
Bettmann, 50, 51, 129, 131; Philip James Corwin, 57; John and Lisa Merrill, 59; Paul A. Souders, 61,
95, 136; Jim Cummins, 64; Tim McGuire, 68; James L. Amos, 69; Grafton Marshall Smith, 81;
Louie Psihoyes, 86; Lois Ellen Frank, 89; Dave Bartruff, 91; David Samuel Robbins, 92; Joel W. Rogers,
94; Tim Thompson, 97; Craig Tuttle, 98; Philip Gendreau, 99; Darrell Gulin, 107 (T); Pat O'Hara,
107(B); Joe McDonald, 110; Doug Wilson, 115; John McAnulty, 117; Jason Hunt, 121; Roger
Ressmeyer, 123; Dan Lamont, 125; Douglas Kent, 127; Corbis, 45; *Alamy:* Chuck Pefley, 17;
Steven J Kazlowski, 25; World Foto, 60; D. Hurst, 67; Danita Delimont, 119; *Dembinsky Photo
Associates:* Carl R. Sams, 21; Claudia Adams, 111; *The Image Works:* Barry Sweet, 75; David R.
Frazier, 82; Momatiuk Eastcott, 88; Andre Jenny, 135; *Getty Images:* Natalie Fobes/The Image
Bank, 28; M.L. Harris/Iconia, 30; Roger Werth/Time Life Picutres, 52; Karen Moskowitz, 54;
Glen Allison, 84; *North Wind Picture Archives:* 32, 37, 38; *The Granger Collection:* 35, 41.

Printed in Malaysia
1 3 5 6 4 2

Contents

Washington is layer upon layer of history.

"I remember it rained awful hard that day . . . and the last glimpse I had of them was the women standing under the trees with their wet bonnets over their faces and their aprons to their eyes."

—description of pioneer families arriving in 1851

"In the late 1800s when the railroad was being built out here, my great-uncle left his home in South Dakota and came west. . . . Well, the end of the line for my great-uncle was right here in Washington. He loved it so much that he didn't want to go back to Dakota; they had to come get him."

—Reverend Paul Gross, who moved to Washington in 1960

"The sacred salmon runs are in decline. It is the moral duty, therefore, of the Indian people of the Columbia River to see them restored. We have to take care of them so that they can take care of us. Entwined together inextricably, no less now than ever before, are the fates of both the salmon and the Indian people."

—Ted Strong, Yikama Nation, 1997

Its people have big plans for the future.

"The Pacific age is coming, and the Northwest is right on the edge of it. I'm studying Chinese—everything's going to be happening between here and China."

—fifteen-year-old Dave Rickhart

"A new century is coming at us like a bullet train. And it's up to us to either rise to challenges or watch as that train passes by."

—Governor Gary Locke, 1997

"We're really competing with other countries. We happen to be the most trade-dependent state in the nation—one in three jobs directly or indirectly.

So we have to see our economic future in our trade relationships with all those other countries."

—Governor Christine Gregoire, 2006

The state's natural beauty appeals to both residents and visitors . . .

"The mountain itself can be buried in dark clouds any time of the year. And on many days, the land below falls away emerald and juicy, and water runs in streams out of the snowpack lying carelessly around. In the middle of summer, the meadows, which spread in waves away and away from the trails below the glaciers, are bedewed with lilies and asters, buttercup and Indian paintbrush, and a dozen other blossoms. . . ."

—writer Sallie Tisdale, describing Mount Rainier in *Stepping Westward*

. . . but the people of Washington are trying to find a balance between economic growth and environmental protection.

"Power and Fish—You Can Have Both!"

—hydropower industry poster from the 1940s

"You have to keep your eye on the goal. We want to have as many kinds of wildlife habitat as we can support out here."

—Robert Kent, former manager of the Columbia Basin Wildlife Areas

From green hills lapped by the blue Pacific to golden brown interior plains, Washington is a state of contradictions. Rain forest and sunbaked outback. Big city and small town. Logger and environmentalist. Urban trendsetter and range-riding cowboy. Blessed—or cursed—with a reputation as one of America's best places to live, Washington draws people from around the world. Newcomers and old-timers alike have visions of what the state should be. Their challenge is to find a vision that all can share.

Chapter One

Some of Everything

"There is a trail that encircles the mountain," wrote Roger Toll in 1920. "It is a trail that leads through primeval forests, close to the mighty glaciers, past waterfalls and dashing torrents, up over ridges, and down into canyons; it leads through a veritable wonderland of beauty and grandeur."

Toll, the superintendent of Mount Rainier National Park, was referring to a new trail that work crews had built on the mountain. The footpath wound all the way around Rainier, close to timberline, the place where forest gives way to high-altitude meadows and open slopes of rock and ice. It had been created to make it easier for park rangers to patrol for fires and illegal hunting on all sides of the mighty, snowcapped peak. Soon, though, word of the remarkable landscape along the trail was drawing hikers to Mount Rainier. Now known as the Wonderland Trail, the 93-mile-long path lets thousands of people each year experience the variety and majesty of wild Washington.

A popular way to explore Mount Rainier National Park is along its Wonderland Trail.

Washington owes its wide variety of landscapes to the chain of mountains that runs through it, splitting it into two parts, the east side and the west side. Those mountains are the Cascades, the state's backbone. The tallest peak is Mount Rainier, at 14,410 feet. On clear days Rainier's broad-shouldered, white-topped dome can be seen from many miles away, glowing pink and gold at sunrise or sunset.

Northeastern Washington, called the Okanogan Highlands, is covered with low, rugged mountains that spread into Canada and Idaho. South of

the highlands is the Columbia Plateau, a high, dry prairie that covers much of southeastern Washington. The plateau is a giant lava bed—one of the largest and thickest in the world. Thousands of years ago volcanoes spilled layer after layer of lava across the land. Later, enormous floods rushed across it, carving deep, narrow trenches called coulees. Along Washington's southeastern border is the Palouse, a region of gently rolling, rounded hills covered with a thick, fertile layer of windblown soil. The fields of the Palouse, where wheat and dry peas are grown, throw a quilt of vivid colors over the land.

Mount Rainier is the highest volcano in the Cascade Mountains.

Contour farming of wheat fields creates a dramatic landscape in the hilly Palouse region of Washington.

Washington's largest river, the Columbia, flows south from Canada, sweeping through central Washington in a huge loop before it flows west into the Pacific. The lower Columbia marks the state's border with Oregon. The Columbia was once one of America's mightiest rivers, a rushing torrent with many waterfalls and rapids. Dams have slowed its flow and turned it into a string of sluggish lakes. The dams provide water to irrigate the plateau and the Palouse. They also produce hydroelectric power for industries and homes throughout the Pacific Northwest.

If you climbed a high peak in the Cascades and looked down at the western third of Washington, you would see a patchwork of green and blue, a mixture of land and water. The Skykomish, Skagit, Snoqualmie, and dozens of other rivers tumble down the mountain slopes to the Puget Sound Lowland, a flat strip of land sandwiched between the Cascades and the jumbled geography of the state's western edge. Nearly three-quarters of Washington's people live in the Puget Sound Lowland.

In the north the lowland curves around Puget Sound, a long, deep arm of the Pacific Ocean that cuts into the heart of Washington. Centuries ago huge ice sheets called glaciers crawled over this land, carving channels into it. When the ice retreated, the sea flowed into the channels and created the maze of waterways that is the sound. Hundreds of islands dot its surface. Some are merely craggy boulders holding a single tree above the water. Others are home to large communities.

Deception Pass Bridge connects islands in Puget Sound.

LAND AND WATER

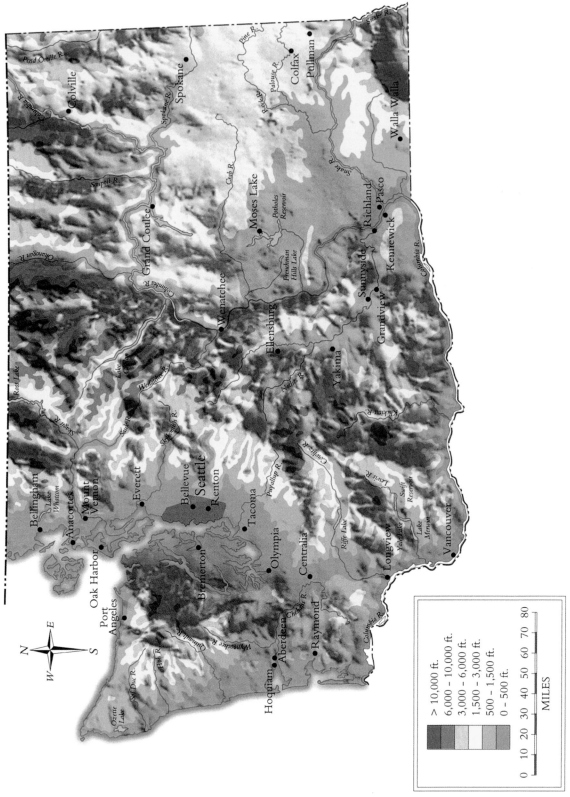

Pond Oreille R.

Colville

Columbia R.

Sanpoil R.

Okanogan R.

Spokane R.

Spokane

Grand Coulee

Crab R.

Moses Lake

Columbia R.

Wenatchee

Lake Chelan

Wenatchee R.

Ellensburg

Naches R.

Stilaguamish R.

Ross Lake

Skagit R.

Bellingham

Lake Whatcom

Anacortes

Mount Vernon

Oak Harbor

Port Angeles

Soleduc R.

Ozette Lake

Sol Duc R.

Elwha R.

Quinault R.

Wynoochee R.

Hoquiam

Aberdeen

Chehalis R.

Raymond

Skykomish R.

Snoqualmie R.

Everett

Bellevue Seattle Renton

Bremerton

Tacoma

Olympia

Centralia

Puyallup R.

Riffe Lake

Cowlitz R.

Yakima

Kittitas R.

Lewis R.

Swift Reservoir

Yale Lake

Lake Merwin

Longview

Vancouver

Columbia R.

Pine R.

Colfax

Pullman

Snake R.

Palouse R.

Rock R.

Walla Walla

Snake R.

Richland Pasco

Potholes Reservoir

Freuchman Hills Lake

Sunnyside Kennewick

Grandview

Columbia R.

A LEGEND CROSSES THE COLUMBIA RIVER

A thousand years ago a huge landslide blocked the Columbia River. Over time the river washed out the base of this "dam," leaving a natural bridge of earth and rock connecting the two banks.

The Chinook Indians called this bridge the Bridge of the Gods and said that the Great Spirit had placed two of his sons, in the form of mountains, on either side of the bridge—Klickitat on the north and Wyeast on the south. All went well until the beautiful Squaw Mountain moved into the neighborhood. Although she loved Wyeast, she liked to flirt with Klickitat. Soon the brothers were fighting over her, stamping and spitting fire and ash into the air and hurling rocks across the river at one another. Their rumblings shook the Bridge of the Gods so hard that it crumbled into the river.

Klickitat was bigger than Wyeast, and he won the battle. Wyeast gave up Squaw Mountain, who sadly took her place at Klickitat's side. But because she still loved Wyeast, she went to sleep and never woke up. To this day Klickitat stands over her with bowed head.

The mountains that the Native Americans called sons of the Great Spirit are volcanoes in the Cascades. Wyeast is Oregon's Mount Hood. Klickitat is Washington's Mount Adams. Squaw Mountain is just west of Mount Adams. And today the Bridge of the Gods is a highway bridge across the Columbia River. Every day hundreds of cars, trucks, and bicycles cross between Washington and Oregon on this bridge, which opened in 1926.

West of the sound is the Olympic Peninsula, where jagged mountains with snow-sprinkled peaks form Seattle's skyline. A smaller peninsula, the Kitsap, juts like a thumb from the Olympic Peninsula into Puget Sound. The highest peak in the Olympic Mountains is Mount Olympus, at nearly 8,000 feet. When its veil of clouds lifts, Olympus is visible from Vancouver Island, a part of Canada separated from the Olympic Peninsula by a waterway called the Strait of Juan de Fuca.

South of the dramatic Olympic Peninsula is the gentler landscape of southwestern Washington. Ranges of hills, with quiet farming valleys nestled between them, stretch down to the bays and beaches of the coast. The two largest bays are Grays Harbor, with the cities of Hoquiam and Aberdeen on its northern edge, and Willapa Bay, famous for its oysters and the quiet beauty of its marshy shores. The Pacific Northwestern writer Ivan Doig called the Willapa Bay area a "misty, oozeful kind of place." In the far southwest is Long Beach Peninsula, a 28-mile strip of sand dotted with piles of salt-strained driftwood washed ashore over the years by the ceaseless wind and waves.

At 28 miles, Long Beach is one of the longest beaches in the United States.

"Washington has two completely different climates," says the Seattle weather scientist Doug McCleary. "Our weather machine has two main parts—the Pacific Ocean and the Cascade Mountains." Powerful winds from the Pacific blow moisture toward Washington. When the moisture hits land, it falls as rain or snow. Onrushing clouds get stuck against the Olympic Mountains and drop their moisture there, making the west side of the Olympic Peninsula the wettest part of Washington. Some places average 135 inches of rain a year.

But plenty of moisture makes it past the Olympics. The Puget Sound Lowland—including Seattle, Washington's largest city—gets about 40 inches of rain a year. Most of it falls between October and April in frequent drizzles that can go on for days. "It gets kind of weird," admitted teenager Kariah Mills, who moved to Seattle from Michigan. "It's not very cold here in the winter, which is nice, but sometimes I really miss the sun. Day after day of gray skies can drive you crazy. And people here don't use umbrellas. It's like they're trying to pretend it's not raining." That's exactly what they're doing, according to seventeen-year-old Jackson Rewell, who has spent his whole life in Seattle. "You just have to ignore it and get on with your life," he advised. "Sports, hanging out, whatever you want to do. What's the worst that can happen? You get wet."

The western slopes of the Cascades catch a lot of rain and snow. Occasionally Mount Rainier gets more than 1,000 inches in a year. Mount Baker to the north holds the world record for average annual snowfall. Highways through the mountains are frequently closed in winter. But east of the mountains, some places are almost deserts. Parts of the Columbia Plateau get only 6 inches of rain and snow a year.

Rain does not keep this Washingtonian from strolling along Puget Sound.

Coastal Washington is warmer in the winter and cooler in the summer than places farther inland. That's because moist air blowing in from the Pacific keeps temperatures from reaching extremes. Seattle has an average midwinter temperature of about 41 degrees Fahrenheit and a midsummer temperature of about 66 °F. But east of the Cascades, where the air is dryer, temperatures have plunged as low as 48 °F in winter and risen to a broiling 118 °F in summer.

Having one climate west of the mountains and another in the east gives Washingtonians some variety. During the winter people from the east side can go to the cloudy, moist west side for relief from the bitter cold of the plateau, while westsiders desperate for a glimpse of the sun can spend a weekend happily shivering in the bright but chilly interior.

WILD WASHINGTON

Trees once covered more than half of Washington. Large areas have been cut to create farmland or to harvest timber, but enough of the state remains forested to earn it the nickname the Evergreen State.

Most of Washington's trees are evergreens—trees that do not shed their leaves in the fall. The dry east side has forests of ponderosa pine, especially in the mountainous north. It also has big, treeless stretches of high-prairie vegetation, such as mile upon mile of sweet-scented gray green sagebrush. The state tree, the western hemlock, grows all over Washington, as does the Douglas fir. The largest trees and densest forests are in the western Cascades and the Olympics, where dark green ferns and moss dripping with moisture form a lush undergrowth beneath the high canopies of western red cedar and Sitka spruce.

Flowers are one of Washington's glories. More than three thousand kinds of wildflowers grow in the state. Mountain meadows and eastern roadsides blaze with pink fireweed, red Indian paintbrush, purple lupine, and yellow poppy. One of the most spectacular flowering plants is the coast rhododendron, the state flower. This bush's leaves are glossy green all year long, and its springtime blooms are white, red, yellow, pink, or orange.

Springtime wildflowers bloom in Mount Rainier National Park creating a sea of color.

Wild creatures are plentiful in Washington. Black bear, elk, and deer live in most large forests. Shaggy, white, nimble-footed mountain goats live in some high crags, and cougars dwell in the Cascades and the Olympics. Coyote, bobcat, beaver, fox, otter, and raccoon are native to much of the state.

A mountain goat navigates with ease a ridge in Olympic National Park.

THE GRAY GHOST RETURNS

Gray wolves, also called timber wolves, once roamed through Washington's mountains, slipping soft-footed through the forests and making the night skies ring with their clear, long-drawn howls. Then hunters and settlers came.

Beginning in the 1820s fur trappers carried out a busy traffic in wolf pelts. In the early 1900s the U.S. government wiped out the state's remaining wolves, which farmers and ranchers called pests. But in 1991 biologists in the North Cascades saw a pack of gray wolves. The next year a pack appeared farther south. Wildlife experts believe that wolves from Canada may be slowly moving into the wilder parts of the Cascades. The Washington Department of Fish and Wildlife has even considered a project to reintroduce wolves to the Olympic Peninsula.

Wolves are an endangered species in Washington. The law forbids people to kill or even bother them. But will wolves harm humans? Wolves disappear quickly once they sense people. "There has never been a report of a healthy wild wolf in North America seriously injuring a human being," said Ed Bans of the U.S. Fish and Wildlife Service. "Think about Canadians—twenty-five million of them live with 60,000 wolves, and there's never been a case where a wolf has attacked a small child in a red cape by a school bus stop." In other words, Little Red Riding Hood has nothing to fear if wolves reclaim their place in our northern forests.

The bald eagle is one of hundreds of kinds of birds that live in Washington or pass through it while migrating. Several hundred eagles spend time along the Skagit River north of Seattle, and in late winter people take boat trips to watch them gather in trees and snatch fish from the water. On the east side bird-watchers flock to the Columbia National Wildlife Refuge in Othello to see a rare colony of sandhill cranes—tall, gangly birds that dance to attract mates. "Washington is a birder's paradise," a bird-watcher from Everett proclaimed. "One year I even saw snowy owls from Alaska feeding along the coast."

Washington's best-known sea creatures may be orcas, black-and-white whales that frolic in Puget Sound and the Strait of Juan de Fuca. People on ferryboats that run between the mainland and the islands sometimes see these mighty mammals leaping from the water. Gray whales cruise the deeper offshore waters. Washington's rivers and seas are home to many varieties of salmon and trout. Clam, oyster, crab, and lobster live in the coastal waters. "Puget Sound is an underwater wonderland," said Bill Sayre, a scuba diving instructor. "I've dived all around the world, and no place is better than here. The water is cold, but you see so many wonderful things. Especially the octopuses. They're everywhere, big ones, small ones. I've even seen them living in old bottles. They are shy, smart, and fascinating to watch."

ENVIRONMENTAL ISSUES

Some of Washington's living things are in trouble. Washington's Department of Fish and Wildlife (WDFW) lists animal and plant species the state has identified as endangered (meaning that they are at risk of becoming extinct) or threatened (meaning that they could easily become endangered). As of fall 2006 Washington had twenty-nine species of endangered animals.

An orca breaches in the waters off the San Juan Islands.

Seven were whales: sei, blue, fin, humpback, sperm, black right, and orca. The gray wolf, pygmy rabbit, Columbian white-tailed deer, woodland caribou, leatherback sea turtle, and brown pelican were considered endangered by both state and federal wildlife agencies. Three butterfly species were endangered: the Oregon silverspot butterfly, the Mardon skipper, and the Taylor's checkerspot. Several dozen other species of animals and plants were either endangered, threatened, or declining.

When a species' survival is on the line, the WDFW makes a plan to protect it. Sadly, time has already run out for the pygmy rabbit. These tiny, ground-burrowing creatures, the smallest rabbits in North America, live in dry, sagebrush regions of Washington and seven other western states. Washington's pygmy rabbits, sometimes called Columbia pygmy rabbits, formed a subgroup that was slightly different from those in the other states. The rabbit's numbers dropped sharply during the second half of the twentieth century, as farming and land development gobbled up its sagebrush habitat.

In 1995 fewer than 250 of the native rabbits remained in Washington. The WDFW developed a plan to preserve habitat areas. It also took sixteen rabbits from the wild, hoping that a captive breeding program would produce young rabbits that could be released into the wild. But by 2003 the number of rabbits in the wild had dwindled to about thirty, and the captive breeding program was less successful than scientists had hoped. Then, in 2006 the last captive male Columbia pygmy rabbit died—and wildlife experts found no trace of surviving Columbia pygmy rabbits in the wild. Two female Columbia pygmy rabbits remain, but without a male, the species cannot survive in purebred form. Wildlife managers now hope to breed the surviving females with pygmy rabbits from Idaho. If they succeed, some of the genetic heritage of Washington's own pygmy rabbits will live on.

Washington's Department of Fish and Wildlife plans on breeding Idaho pygmy rabbits (above) with the two remaining Columbia pygmy in hopes of creating hybrid offspring.

Washingtonians are looking for ways to balance economic needs and environmental protection in a number of issues. One involves the state's forests. The timber industry has been a big part of the economy for most of the state's history. Many families' livelihood comes from jobs in the industry, either logging in the forests or operating the sawmills that turn timber into lumber or wood pulp for papermaking. Yet years of clear-cutting—stripping every tree from a section of land—have left some of Washington's hillsides checkerboarded with large, bare patches of stumps. Many clear-cuts scar the state's national forests, right up to the borders of Olympic and Mount Rainier National Parks.

Roadside trees hide the many acres of clear cut stumps on the Olympic Penisula.

Environmentalists point out that even when timber companies plant new trees in a clear-cut, they cannot reproduce a natural forest, which has trees of many ages. "Replanting clear-cuts does nothing but create tree farms," says Michael Hayes of Greenpeace, an environmental organization. Timber industry officials, though, feel that they are doing a good job of replacing forest resources. They believe that clear-cutting is the most efficient method of logging, and logging is needed both for jobs and to meet the demand for wood products.

Some of the most bitter fights have been about old-growth forests, places where the trees have never been cut. Some old-growth trees are more than six hundred years old. Loggers love old-growth timber for its high quality, but environmentalists want to preserve and study old-growth forests, because they cannot be replaced. "Once old-growth forests are cut," Hayes pointed out, "they are gone forever." Timber companies are free to cut old growth on private land, although such forests have become rare. Environmental groups try to block logging in old-growth forests on public land with lawsuits and protests. The federal government is working to create a timber policy that will satisfy both groups, but has had little success so far.

Salmon are at the heart of another environmental crisis. Washington's waters once teemed with these fish, which spend part of their lives in freshwater streams and part in the ocean. The salmon industry created thousands of jobs on fishing boats and in canning plants. But each year wild salmon become scarcer. Dams block their migration routes and kill as many as three-quarters of all young salmon when they try to swim to the sea. Soil runoff from clear-cuts muddies the streams where the salmon breed, preventing them from reproducing. Chemicals used on farms and on urban parks and suburban lawns also make their way into the streams, poisoning the salmon. Some streams that used to produce thousands of salmon each year now produce only a few or none at all. Washingtonians, however, are taking steps to protect and restore streams. For example, they have enacted new rules about the levels of certain chemicals allowed in waterways. And builders who plan to pave large parking lots must construct systems to control the water that runs off these hard surfaces. This helps prevent erosion as well as keeping pollution from automotive chemicals from reaching the waterways.

Sockeye salmon swim upstream to breeding grounds.

As the number of salmon has gone down, the demand for them has gone up. The government now sets limits on the number of salmon taken each year, but the salmon population continues to decline. The WDFW is working with federal and state environmental agencies and representatives of the fishing and timber industries to balance the competing needs of businesses, workers, and species survival. It hopes to work out a plan that will let people keep catching the fish while still saving enough to provide salmon for the future. Like the timber issue, however, the salmon problem is very difficult to solve. "Everyone knows there's a crisis, but no one knows what to do," said fisherman Tony Gonsalves. "Some people want to blow up the dams; some want to ban fishing for thirty years. The trouble is, no one knows whether any of these ideas will work." The WDFW calls the salmon problem "one of the state's overriding environmental challenges."

Environmental issues often seem to turn one part of the state against another—east against west, or city dwellers against country folk. "People in Seattle don't understand our problems," said a logger in the small town of Pateros. "They come into the mountains and see the trees and get all excited, and then they go back to their offices and condos while we hope we don't get laid off before we can buy winter coats for our kids." Lovers of forest and wildlife have realized that they cannot save the forests or the salmon until they admit that people also need help. "My job is to bring all sides together and try to find a way for everyone to gain something," said a supervisor in the state's environmental office. "We're all in this state together, and we've got to solve its problems together."

Chapter Two

Linking Past and Future

People have been living in Washington for 12,000 years, and perhaps even longer. Native Americans, explorers, pioneers, builders, and dreamers have woven the pattern of Washington's human history.

THE NATIVE AMERICANS

Dozens of Native-American tribes lived in Washington before European explorers arrived. Their cultures fell into two broad groups. East of the Cascade Mountains lived the peoples of the interior, or inner part of the region. West of the mountains lived the peoples of the coast.

Interior Tribes

East of the Cascades, in the dry forests of the Okanogan Highlands and the grasslands of the Palouse and the Columbia Plateau, lived the Nez Perce, Cayuse, Okanogan, Colville, Spokane, and Yakima (also spelled Yakama) peoples. These communities moved often. When they traveled, people walked while dogs pulled their goods on sledges made of poles. Families lived in pit houses—shallow holes with grass or branch roofs—or dwellings made of woven mats.

Native peoples of the Northwest Coast carved totem poles that told a family's story and identified the pole's owner.

The women gathered seeds and wild plants, especially sweet purple huckleberries and the nutritious root of the camas lily. The men hunted deer, elk, and small game, such as rabbit. When they camped near lakes, they caught fish and ducks. But the most important food for these Native Americans was salmon. Using nets and traps made of poles and woven plants, they harvested salmon as the fish came up the rivers and streams to breed. The Native Americans feasted on fresh salmon. They dried strips of fish over fires or in the sun to provide food for the winter. They also made pemmican, nutritious and long-lasting cakes of pounded meat, fish oil, and berries.

Native Americans catch salmon, a staple of their diet.

Trade played a vital part in the lives of the Plateau tribes and also of the Chinook people, who lived along the Columbia River. Native Americans brought trade goods into what is now eastern and central Washington from three directions: Idaho and the Great Plains of Montana, Wyoming, and the Dakotas to the east; the forests of Puget Sound and the Pacific Coast to the west; and central Oregon, Nevada, and California to the south. At special market villages or gatherings throughout the Plateau region and along the Columbia, local tribes exchanged their own goods—such as dried food, skins, stone tools, and woven baskets—for shells and crafts from the coast and for bison hides from the plains. The peoples of the Plateau and the Columbia were a key part of a far-reaching Native-American trade network that moved goods between the center of the continent and the Northwest Coast.

In the early eighteenth century the Plains tribes brought something new to the Native Americans of interior Washington: horses. Brought to North America by the Spanish, horses changed the lives of many Native-American peoples in the West, including such groups as the Colville, Nez Perce, and Yakima. Horses allowed them to travel farther and faster in their quest for food. And with horses to carry or haul their possessions, some of the interior groups adopted a custom of the Plains Indians and began living in tepees, tents made of hides draped over poles, which they carried from place to place.

Coastal Tribes

West of the mountains Washington's Native-American peoples settled along the coasts of Puget Sound, the Olympic Peninsula, and the bays and beaches south of the peninsula. Among the Puget Sound groups were the Nisqually, Puyallup, Nooksack, Skagit, and Tulalip. The Pacific Coast was home to such tribes as the Makah, Hoh, Muckleshoot, Lummi, Quinault, and Chehalis.

The coastal peoples lived in an area rich in natural resources. They lived in permanent villages. These were often located at the mouths of streams, which provided sources of freshwater near the fishing grounds at sea. Houses were large and sturdy, and made of wooden planks, usually cedar. When coastal peoples made seasonal migrations to food sources such as camas fields, berry grounds, or fishing stations, they sometimes took the planks from these houses with them for use in frames at other sites. People made clothing from strips of cedar bark, wore furs or skins for extra warmth, and wove basketlike hats for rain protection. With fire and tools they hollowed out the trunks of giant cedars and shaped them into seagoing canoes.

Salmon was a key ingredient of the coastal peoples' diet, but people also caught herring, halibut, and other fish using nets, fish traps, spears, and fishing lines. Some groups, such as the Makah, hunted seal and whales from their canoes. As with the interior tribes, women gathered berries, roots, and other wild foods. They also grew potatoes and tended clam beds.

Western Washington's abundant resources and mild climate gave the coastal Indians a comfortable life. They used their leisure time to create some of the finest arts and crafts of Native America, including towering totem poles of carved and painted wood and finely decorated baskets of woven cedar strips.

The coastal tribes also developed a highly structured social system in which people were very much aware of their class, or ranking in the group. The biggest class distinction was between free people and slaves (mostly captured in raids, but sometimes enslaved because of debt). Some groups also divided free people into aristocrats and commoners. Communities were ruled by chieftains, and the senior men and women organized and supervised such economic activities as fishing, hunting, and trading.

The coastal peoples were the first of Washington's Native Americans to have contact with Europeans. These newcomers were few and far between at first, but in time they became a flood that washed over the Indian lands.

THE EXPLORERS

The outside world began exploring Washington in the second half of the eighteenth century, when Spanish, Portuguese, Russian, British, French, and American vessels probed the Pacific coastline of North America. Some of the San Juan Islands in Puget Sound are still called by names given to them by Spanish sea captains.

The English were the next to arrive. In 1778 the explorer James Cook sailed along the coast. While Cook studied and mapped the coast, his men obtained a number of sea otter skins. Later, when Cook sailed to China, they sold these furs at high prices. Soon the fur trade was booming.

The first American vessel to arrive on the Washington coast was the *Columbia*, captained by Robert Gray. In 1792 Gray sailed into the mouth of the great river that he named after his ship. That same year a British naval explorer named George Vancouver reached Washington's waters. Vancouver spent two years exploring Puget Sound, charting its islands, and naming places after his friends and crewmen—Rainier, Puget, and Baker. Members of his crew spread the word about the region's beauty and abundant resources. One of them, Joseph Whidbey, called it "a country equal to any in the world."

Native Americans greet the Columbia *on the river that was named after the ship.*

As a result of these voyages both Great Britain and the United States laid claim to the Pacific Northwest Coast. To strengthen the American claim, President Thomas Jefferson sent Meriwether Lewis and William Clark west in 1804 to explore the land between the Mississippi River and the Pacific Ocean. The Lewis and Clark expedition crossed the Rocky Mountains and then followed the Snake and Columbia rivers to the ocean. The explorers returned east with word of the rich, fertile territory they had seen along the Columbia. Fur trappers and later settlers turned their attention to "the Oregon country," the vast region that included present-day Oregon, Washington, and Idaho.

THE PIONEERS

The first English and American pioneers came for fur, especially the soft beaver pelts that were used to make hats and coats. These furs became so valuable during the 1800s that they were exchanged like money. A British firm called the North West Company sent men into the Oregon country to buy furs from the Native Americans, and in 1810 they built Spokane House, a trading post near where the city of Spokane stands today. It was the first white settlement in what is now Washington.

Americans built Fort Okanogan, a trading post similar to Spokane House, in 1811. That same year a group of American traders, investors, and adventurers built Fort Astoria at the mouth of the Columbia River. Great Britain and the United States went to war in 1812, and the following year the British seized Fort Astoria and renamed it Fort George. After the war ended, Great Britain and the United States signed the Treaty of Ghent. One term of the treaty was that Oregon, as the region on both sides of the Columbia was called, would be shared by the two nations. It was not clear which country would eventually own the region.

Fort Okanogan was built as a fur-trading establishment in 1811.

At first it seemed that the English would control the region. The powerful Hudson's Bay Company (HBC), an English trading firm operating in Canada, sent men into Washington in 1821. Four years later John McLoughlin built an HBC fort on the north bank of the Columbia River and named it Fort Vancouver. Although McLoughlin was supposed to look after England's interests in the Oregon country, he helped Americans get settled there. Many American pioneers owed their success—and their lives—to his good advice and generosity.

Some of the first Americans to travel overland to Washington were missionaries who came to preach Christianity to the Native Americans. In 1836 missionaries led by Marcus and Narcissa Whitman founded an outpost near present-day Walla Walla. According to the author Roger Sale, "When they failed to convert the native people in satisfying numbers, they sought to attract American settlers to fill their pews."

The Whitman party's route across the continent soon became a highway for hundreds, then thousands of settlers who came west with wagons and livestock to start new lives and establish new communities. "People talk a lot about the Oregon Trail, or even the Oregon and California Trail," said Lynn Halsemeier, a teacher in Tacoma. "Let's not forget that that same trail also brought a lot of folks to Washington."

Settlers traveled across the Oregon and California trails to establish new towns and communities in the Pacific Northwest.

Fur had brought the traders, but land drew the settlers west. In many parts of the United States good farmland was already scarce and expensive, but in the Oregon country it was free to anyone willing to work and live on it. Pioneers began settling the region around Puget Sound. They founded Tumwater, Washington's first town, in 1845. Olympia came into being a year later.

By this time the United States and Great Britain had decided to divide the Oregon country. The British wanted the Columbia River to serve as the border between British and American territory. The Americans objected. Early in the 1840s an American naval officer and explorer named Charles Wilkes had studied the Pacific Northwest Coast and decided that the Columbia River was too dangerous to be a useful port. Wilkes urged the U.S. government to demand a more northerly border so that Americans would control Puget Sound, with its good ports. In 1846 the two nations agreed on the border that now divides the United States and Canada.

Once the Oregon country belonged to the United States, it was more attractive than ever to American settlers. Not even tragedy slowed them down. The tragedy began with the region's Native Americans, who were dying in great numbers from diseases introduced by the newcomers, especially measles and smallpox. The Indians also began to fear, quite rightly, that they would be shoved off their land to make room for farms and ranches. In 1847 a band of Cayuse Indians, blaming the whites at the Whitman mission for causing the sicknesses among their people, attacked the mission, killing the Whitmans and a dozen others. The Cayuse War that followed pitted American settlers against Native Americans, but it did not discourage other Americans from following the trail west.

A PIONEER WOMAN'S DIARY

Born in Maine in 1811, Mary Richardson started keeping a diary when she was twenty-two years old—and kept it for fifty-seven years. In 1838 she married Elkanah Walker, and they started out on the long and difficult Oregon Trail. Mary Richardson Walker's diary gives glimpses of life on the trail.

April 27. I feel that dangers & perils await; that we ought to realize that every day may be our last.

July 6. We were again saluted by a company on foot. . . . Their faces were painted. White men acted like Indians. It is said that many of the white men in the Mts. try to act as much like Indians as they can & would be glad if they really were so.

July 15. On our right, snow capped mountains. Saw a flock of antelopes. Last night a large band of buffalow passed so near we could hear them pant. Fell in with a company of Snakes [Indians]. Encamped to trade with them . . .

August 25. We descended a longer hill than I ever walked down before. Connor's wife [had a baby]. At noon she collected fuel & prepared dinner. Gave birth to a daughter before sunset.

August 29. Left baggage behind, and hasten on. . . . Arrived at Dr. Whitman about two p.m. . . . Just as we were sitting down to eat melons, the house became thronged with Indians & we were obliged to suspend eating & shake hands with some 30, 40, or 50 of them. Towards night we partook of a fine dinner of vegetables, salt salmon, bread, butter, cream, &c. Thus our long toilsome journey at length came to a close.

STATEHOOD

In 1848 Congress officially made the Pacific Northwest part of the United States by creating the Oregon Territory, with its capital at Oregon City in present-day Oregon. Two years later the government counted a total of 13,000 Americans living in the territory. Less than one-tenth of them lived in what is now Washington.

Although their numbers were small, the settlers living north of the Columbia River were eager to have their own government, for they did not like having to cross the river and travel south to Salem for all official business. They asked Congress to make their region into a separate territory called Columbia. In 1853 Congress created the new territory but named it Washington in honor of the first president.

Between 1853 and 1860 Washington's non–Native-American population rose from fewer than 4,000 to about 11,500 people. The new territory was already growing fast, thanks to its trees. Newcomers marveled at the size of the mighty forest giants of western Washington. Years later they told of trees so big that eight couples could dance atop the stumps after the trees were cut down. Timber was in demand in many places around the world, and ships could easily access harbors in Puget Sound to load it. The first water-powered sawmill went into business on the sound in 1847. By the 1860s steam mills were humming and clattering around its shores. Towns such as Tacoma grew up around the mills.

Cut lumber awaits shipping on a wharf on the Pacific Coast.

In 1851 a group of pioneers founded a settlement that they named Seattle in honor of a local Suquamish Indian chieftain. Seattle (also spelled Sealth, Seatlh, and See-ahth) is a figure of some mystery. Because his people did not keep written records, we know only legends about his life.

Four years later the government placed the Puget Sound tribes on reservations. Seattle died in 1866 and was buried in Suquamish on the Kitsap Peninsula. From his grave you can look across Puget Sound to Seattle, the largest city in North America named for a Native American.

Although Indians in eastern Washington continued to resist being moved off their land and onto reservations into the 1870s, white settlers took control of the area anyway. Many were ranchers who grazed cattle and sheep on the plains. Farmers knew that eastern Washington, with its good soil and plentiful sunshine, would be excellent farming country—if only it were not so dry. By the 1890s people had begun irrigating by channeling river water through their fields. Soon the region was producing wheat and apple crops.

By that time the town of Spokane was flourishing near the site of the old fur-trading post. It became Washington's second-largest city. Spokane was a hub of what people called the Northwest's "inland empire"—the mining, logging, ranching, and farming region that included eastern Washington and Oregon, Idaho, and Montana.

Railroads changed the landscape and boosted industry all over the United States in the late 1800s, and Washington was no exception. In 1883 the Northern Pacific Company completed a railroad connecting Puget Sound with the East Coast. The people of Tacoma were so happy to have the railroad come to their city that a new business district sprang up near the site chosen for the tracks and station—before the track was even laid. And the people of Yakima were so upset when the track passed north of their town instead of through it that they lifted all the buildings in town and moved them to the railroad line. All across Washington new towns came into being along the tracks.

Trains boosted immigration to Washington, as people discovered that it was a lot easier to get there by railroad than by wagon. By 1889 the territory had more than 300,000 inhabitants. That year was a turning point in Washington's history. The territory became the nation's forty-second state.

The railroad provided an easy and quick means of travel to the West Coast and Seattle (above).

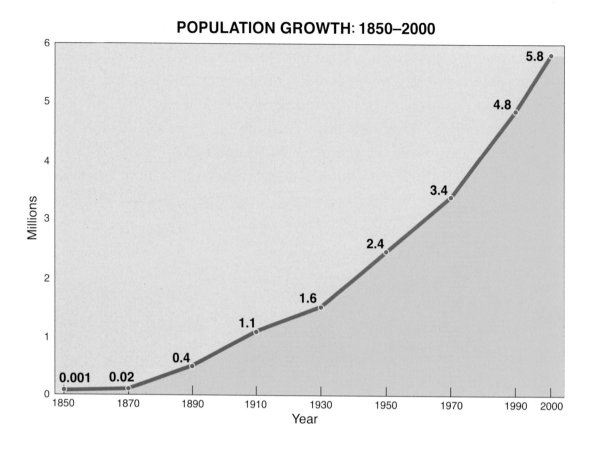

POPULATION GROWTH: 1850–2000

(Millions / Year)

0.001 · 0.02 · 0.4 · 1.1 · 1.6 · 2.4 · 3.4 · 4.8 · 5.8

MODERN WASHINGTON

At the end of the nineteenth century Seattle had a surge of growth spurred by events thousands of miles to the north. Far away in Canada's Klondike region, miners struck gold. The first shipload of the precious metal arrived in Seattle in 1897. When word got out, the Klondike gold rush was on. People from all around the world swarmed to Seattle, fighting to get places on ships headed for Alaska, the gateway to the Klondike. Business in Seattle boomed as merchants sold supplies to the hopeful prospectors.

The growing timber industry fed the boom, employing two out of every three working Washingtonians. But the life of the lumberjack was not easy. As the writer Doug Honig says, "Logging was strenuous physical labor performed outdoors in the rain. . . . After a ten-hour day in the woods, lumberjacks trudged back in wet clothes to crowded, boxlike shacks with neither showers nor drying rooms. . . . The lumberjacks' biggest gripes concerned sleeping conditions. Camps often provided neither blankets nor mattresses, but simply hard pallets with perhaps a bit of straw."

Logging Washington's forests was hard work, but the timber industry fueled the state's economic growth.

ACRES OF CLAMS

The melody of "Acres of Clams" comes from an Irish song about a wandering fiddler, "Rosin the Beau." This same tune has been used many times over with different sets of words. It was a favorite in nineteenth-century presidential campaigns, notably in 1860, as "Lincoln and Liberty."

For one who gets riches by mining,
Perceiving that hundreds grow poor,
I made up my mind to try farming,
The only pursuit that is sure.

Chorus: The only pursuit that is sure,
(2 times)
I made up my mind to try farming,
The only pursuit that is sure.

So, rolling my grub in a blanket,
I left my tools on the ground.
And I started one morning to shank it
For the country they call Puget Sound.

Chorus: For the country . . .

Arriving flat broke in midwinter,
The ground was enveloped in fog;
And covered all over with timber
Thick as hair on the back of a dog.

Chorus: Thick as hair . . .

When I looked at the prospects so
gloomy
The tears trickled over my face;
And I thought that my travels had
brought me
To the end of the jumping-off place.

Chorus: To the end . . .

I staked me a claim in the forest
And set myself down to hard toil.
For two years I chopped and I
struggled,
But I never got down to the soil.

Chorus: But I never . . .

I tried to get out of the country,
But poverty forced me to stay.
Until I became an old settler,
Then nothing could drive me away.

Chorus: Then nothing . . .

And now that I'm used to the country,
I think that if man ever found
A place to live easy and happy,
That Eden is on Puget Sound.

Chorus: That Eden . . .

No longer the slave of ambition.
I laugh at the world and its shams;
As I think of my happy condition,
Surrounded by acres of clams.

Chorus: Surrounded by acres . . .

Workers' demands for improved conditions, shorter hours, and better pay steered Washington toward liberal leaders who tried to help ordinary people and give them a greater voice in government. Washington also showed its progressive side in 1910, when it became the fifth state to give women the right to vote.

One of those who had fought for women's rights was May Arkwright Hutton. She and her husband had invested in an Idaho silver mine and struck it rich. They moved to Spokane in 1906. Hutton devoted her energy to politics, tirelessly writing and making speeches that argued for women's suffrage. Her work on the 1910 campaign helped bring the ballot to Washington women.

Washington contributed ships, timber, wheat, and about 70,000 servicemen and women to the U.S. war effort during World War I, which ended in 1918. In February 1919, just months after the end of the war, Seattle became the site of one of the largest actions in the history of the American labor movement. It started when 35,000 shipyard workers went on strike to demand higher pay. Within a few weeks members of 110 local unions had joined the strike in support of the shipyard workers. Strikers maintained vital services, such as milk delivery, laundry for hospital linens, and fire protection. Otherwise, though, the city was shut down. The strikers ended their action without achieving their goals, but they had shown the power of an organized labor movement.

Prosperity followed World War I, but the good times ended in 1929, when the United States entered the Great Depression, a period of worldwide economic trouble. Times were hard in Washington—in 1933 the unemployment rate stood at an all-time high of 25 percent. As part of a program to give work to the jobless, the federal government employed thousands of Washingtonians on two immense construction projects: the Bonneville

Dam, completed in 1937, and the Grand Coulee Dam, completed in 1941. In addition to controlling water so that the farms and orchards of the Columbia Plateau could be irrigated, the dams made plentiful electrical power available to the region.

In 1941 the United States entered World War II. The war brought many changes to Washington. Some of the changes seemed good. The demand for war materials supported new industries. Shipyards were busy, and thousands of people from around the country found jobs in new plants making airplanes and aluminum.

The Grand Coulee Dam was constructed to control irrigation and flooding, as well as generate power.

Other changes were not so good. The government built a top secret military plant at Hanford in central Washington. Workers there made the plutonium that was used in one of the atomic bombs dropped on Japan. Years later people would learn that leaks of deadly radiation from Hanford were responsible for sicknesses in the area. "The government had no right to do what it did to us," said Aileen Warren, whose family lived in nearby Richland at the time. "It treated people like lab rats."

World War II brought disaster to Japanese Americans living in Washington and all along the West Coast. Fearing that these people might secretly work for Japan, America's enemy in the war, the federal government rounded them up and forced them to spend the war years in "relocation camps" far from their homes. Although most of the Japanese Americans sent

Japanese Americans in Washington board buses bound for internment camps in other states.

to the camps were U.S. citizens, they were treated like criminals—even though they had committed no crime. The camps were really prisons, surrounded by barbed wire and armed guards.

Many Americans of Japanese descent lost everything when they were uprooted from their homes, businesses, and jobs. Some of Washington's Japanese Americans, however, managed to rebuild their lives. Junkoh Harui's family had owned a plant nursery on Bainbridge Island since the early 1900s. When the family had to leave during the war, the gardens fell into ruin. People stole most of the plants. But a few seedlings that Harui's father had planted just before leaving are now strong, 60-foot pines. "My parents had what is called *gaman*—inner strength, the strength to persevere," Harui said. "It's a great legacy for us."

The second half of the twentieth century brought continued growth to Washington. A world's fair in Seattle in 1962 and another in Spokane in 1974 drew attention to the state. Two structures built for the 1962 fair became Seattle landmarks: the Space Needle, which resembles a giant flying saucer perched atop a tower, and the monorail, a train that runs on a single track above downtown's streets.

In 1962 Seattle hosted the World's Fair. New construction included fairgrounds and the famous Space Needle.

People began to speak of Washington as a great place to live—safe, clean, uncrowded, and bursting with natural beauty. In the final years of the twentieth century and the early years of the twenty-first, industries such as electronics, manufacturing, software design, and biotechnology research lured people to the Puget Sound area. Others came to Washington for the mild climate, the scenery, or the relaxed, outdoorsy way of life.

A piece of Washington's scenery erupted on May 18, 1980, thrusting the state into the news around the world. Mount Saint Helens, a volcano in the Cascade Range between Mount Rainier and the Columbia River, blew its top, sending a vast cloud of ash and steam high into the air. Rivers of hot mud poured down the mountainside, ripping trees from the ground and clogging rivers. Fifty-seven people died, and a thick layer of ash fell like gray snow over hundreds of square miles. The ash cloud created such darkness that people in Yakima, in central Washington, had to drive with their headlights on in midday.

A huge tower of smoke escapes the erupting Mount Saint Helens.

The 1980 explosion was a dramatic reminder that Washington's scenic Cascades are volcanoes, and they are still alive. Beneath their surface, lava bubbles and steam hisses. Geologists are working with state, local, and city agencies on creating emergency plans for the next eruption, which is bound to come someday. It could even happen again at Mount Saint Helens, which entered a period of new activity in late 2004. Scientists monitoring Mount Saint Helens over the next couple of years recorded thousands of small earthquakes. Plumes of steam and ash occasionally burst skyward, and a dome of fresh lava rose inside the crater.

In the early 2000s Washington played a key role in a movement to improve security at U.S. ports. After the September 11, 2001, terrorist attacks on New York City and Washington, D.C., concerns arose about the ports—including Seattle and Tacoma—where 1.8 million cargo containers enter the United States each year. Senator Patty Murray of Washington helped create a plan called Operation Safe Commerce that could eventually track each cargo container from the time it is packed abroad to its delivery in the United States. When a bomb scare shut down Seattle Harbor—one of the nation's busiest ports—for three hours in August 2006, Murray declared, "We cannot be passive about the issue of security. We have to be much tougher on it."

Washington's bustling ports, lined with forests of cargo cranes, are a sign of economic health. Despite setbacks and challenges that face every state, Washington's population and economy seem likely to keep growing. Longtime residents and newcomers alike hope that they can keep their state Evergreen.

Chapter Three

Living in the Northwest

"My parents don't like to tell people we're from California," said a fifteen-year-old boy whose family has lived in Seattle for less than a year. "I guess some people here blame Californians for the city getting more crowded and prices going up, and stuff like that. But the kids in my school think it's cool that I moved here from L.A. Half of them came from somewhere else, too."

Washington is growing quickly. About 4.8 million people lived in the state in 1990. By 2000, according to the federal census, that number had increased to 5.9 million. Unofficial estimates placed the population at about 6.3 million in 2005. Much of that growth was due to people moving from other states, drawn by Washington's reputation as one of the nation's best places to live.

A CHANGING ETHNIC LANDSCAPE

Washington has less ethnic diversity than many other states, but that is beginning to change as its Asian and Hispanic populations increase. Still, 5.3 million Washingtonians identify themselves as non-Hispanic whites.

Washingtonians take pride in their culture, heritage, and natural surroundings.

Multiple streams of migration have shaped Washington's present population. The number of new arrivals surged between 1880 and 1920, after the railroads were built and as industry was getting established. Another wave of migration came between the 1940s and the 1960s. In the late 1970s the number of people coming to the state increased again, and it is still growing.

Some Washingtonians are recent arrivals, but others are descendants of early settlers. Most of these people are of German, English, or Scandinavian ancestry. Their heritage is reflected in such places as Seattle's Ballard neighborhood, where many people from Norway, Sweden, Denmark, and Finland settled during the city's early years. The district still has many Scandinavian businesses, restaurants, and residents. A Ballard woman recalled a visit to the neighborhood from the king of Norway: "Now that was exciting!"

VIKINGS ON THE SOUND

In the 1880s Norwegian settlers founded the town of Poulsbo at the head of Liberty Bay on Puget Sound—a location that resembles the narrow, winding fjords of Norway. Each year the town celebrates its Scandinavian heritage with events that draw visitors from all over the region. The Viking Fest in May features Norwegian food, entertainment, and a parade. Teams from California, Washington, Oregon, and Canada compete in the Viking Cup Scandinavian Invitational soccer tournament. The Fourth of July is celebrated with fireworks on the fjord. In mid-November the Yule Fest begins the holiday season in Norwegian style, with the lighting of a Yule log and the arrival of Father Christmas.

A Norwegian flag flies over the Scandinavian Ballard neighborhood.

ETHNIC WASHINGTON

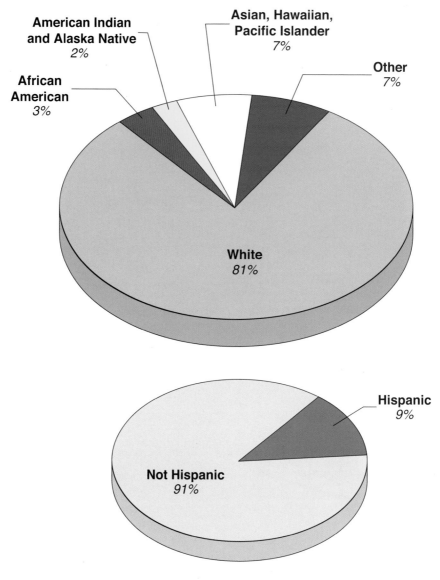

American Indian and Alaska Native
2%

African American
3%

Asian, Hawaiian, Pacific Islander
7%

Other
7%

White
81%

Hispanic
9%

Not Hispanic
91%

Note: A person of Cuban, Mexican, Puerto Rican, South or Central American, or other Spanish culture or origin, regardless of race, is defined as Hispanic.

Chinese and Japanese immigrants were also part of Washington's pioneer history. They worked on railroads and in fisheries, planted orchards, and started businesses. Today the state's Asian population numbers about 320,000 people, and it has become more varied, with significant growth in the numbers of Filipino and Southeast Asian people. Veronica Kim runs a women's health program in Seattle. Her clinic's staff speaks three Chinese dialects, Korean, Tagalog (a language of the Philippines), Vietnamese, Cambodian, Thai, and Laotian. "Even good programs don't work without an interpreter who understands the culture," she said.

Asians have settled in Washington and account for 7 percent of the population.

Washington's first significant number of Hispanics and African Americans arrived during World War II. Although these groups are growing, they still make up only a small part of the state's population: the 2000 census reported 441,509 Hispanics and 199,174 African Americans. "It's really different here," said Carla Mackie, a fourteen-year-old African American whose family moved to

Hispanic dancers are featured at Seattle's Sea Fair Torchlight Parade.

Seattle from the other Washington—the nation's capital. "People here are nice and all, but it's strange to see so few black faces. I feel more like a stranger." As for the Hispanic population, it is small compared to those of some other states, but it is growing. Hispanic Americans from other states, as well as immigrants, frequently get their start in Washington by working in the state's agricultural jobs.

NATIVE WASHINGTON

The 2000 census revealed a population of 96,933 Native Americans in Washington. Most of them belong to one of the twenty-eight tribes that are recognized by the federal government.

About one-third of Washington's Indians live on reservations. These range in size from tiny—such as the territory of the Jamestown S'Klallam, which measures less than one-tenth of a square mile and has sixteen people living in eight houses—to the enormous, such as the 2,187.6-square-mile Yakima Reservation, home to almost 32,000.

Like Native Americans in other parts of the country, some in Washington have learned that gambling casinos—which are permitted by law on Indian-owned territory—can be profitable. According to a report issued in 2006 by the Washington Indian Gaming Association, tribal casinos and other Indian-owned businesses such as shops and restaurants earn more than $3 billion each year. This generates taxes for the state, income for the tribes, and salaries for the four thousand or so Indians who work in the casinos and related businesses (fewer than one-third of casino employees, however, are Native Americans).

The Native Americans of Washington State have done more in recent decades than build casinos. They have also made a strong effort to reclaim their cultural heritage. In the late 1980s Cecilia Eli of the Yakima Reservation lamented the fact that ten local Native-American languages had been lost because reservation schools used to punish students for speaking them. Eli began teaching the traditional languages that she knew to other Native Americans. Her message to her students was, "Never be ashamed of what you are. No matter what people may call you, they cannot take away your Indian blood." Efforts such as hers may help ancient languages, customs, and beliefs survive.

Native-American dancers perform in traditional costume at a powwow at Discovery Park.

KENNEWICK MAN

One of the most famous people in Washington today lived about 9,300 years ago—but he didn't become famous until 1996, when two college students discovered bones adding up to about 80 percent of his skeleton on the bank of the Columbia River near Kennewick.

Scientists were excited. Such ancient human remains are extremely rare in North America. Kennewick Man, as he became known, offered researchers a chance to learn much more about life thousands of years ago. Not everyone shared their excitement, however. Some nearby Native-American tribes wanted the U.S. Army Corps of Engineers, which controlled the remains because they were found on government land, to give the remains to a tribe for burial. They claimed that Kennewick Man was one of their ancestors. "The five tribes have come together and have all said the same thing: These remains need to go back into the ground as soon as possible," declared Armand Minthorn of the Confederated Tribes of the Umatilla.

A group of scientists sued to keep the bones from being buried. They pointed out that it is not certain that Kennewick Man is related to any modern Native Americans, and they felt that the remains should be studied for what they may tell us about the early history of all people. The bones are "rare treasures of humanity," said the scientist Amy Dansie, adding, "We share a common ground. These skeletons are important to remind everybody that we're all one people."

Eventually, the courts determined that no clear link exists between Kennewick Man and the present-day Native-American inhabitants of the region. Scientists were able to begin a detailed examination. Although their research is still going on, they have already made some remarkable finds, such as a 2-inch-long stone spear point embedded in Kennewick Man's pelvis. By comparing mineral stains and other signs on the bones, they have found that Kennewick Man was laid out on his back, with his arms and legs straight—a sign, they say, that he was buried. They hope that future studies will shed light on such things as what he ate and his overall health.

Yet the area's Native American tribes have not given up on Kennewick Man. The Yakima have asked the federal courts to allow them a say in how his bones will be handled after the research is complete. A spokesman says that they still feel "a strong cultural and spiritual connection to those remains."

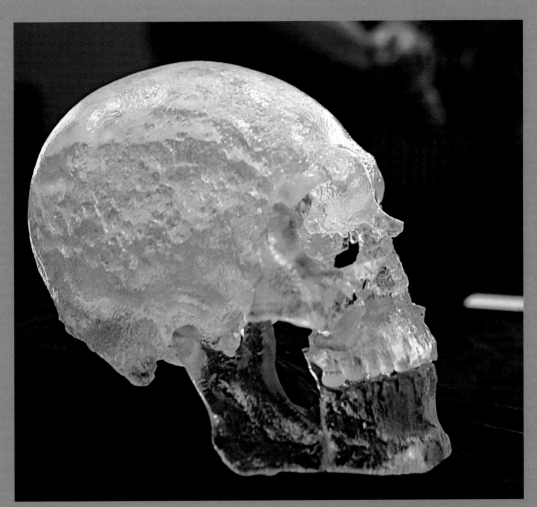

EDUCATION

With Washington's population growing rapidly in recent decades, the state has faced the challenge of keeping its educational system strong while serving an ever-larger number of students. Between 1992 and 2005, for example, the number of young people enrolled in kindergarten through high school in the state's public schools rose by more than 130,000, from 894,756 to 1,025,190.

In 1993 the state adopted a school reform plan that included administering state exams in reading, writing, and math at several grade levels. The goal is to make sure that Washington's students can compete for jobs in the future. In 2005 Washington improved programs to advance learning for young children, made room for eight thousand additional students in its public colleges, and created a $1 billion Life Sciences Discovery Fund to support advanced study and research in health and agriculture. The state also passed a resolution calling for the teaching of tribal histories.

One of Washington's success stories is getting its business community involved in the future of the schools. "The business community believes the single biggest investment in our economy is in education," Governor Christine Gregoire said in 2006, adding that businesses "are going to put millions of dollars on the table to ensure that every child gets quality early childhood education."

Washington's Board of Education's primary goal is to "raise student achievement" throughout the state.

POPULATION DENSITY

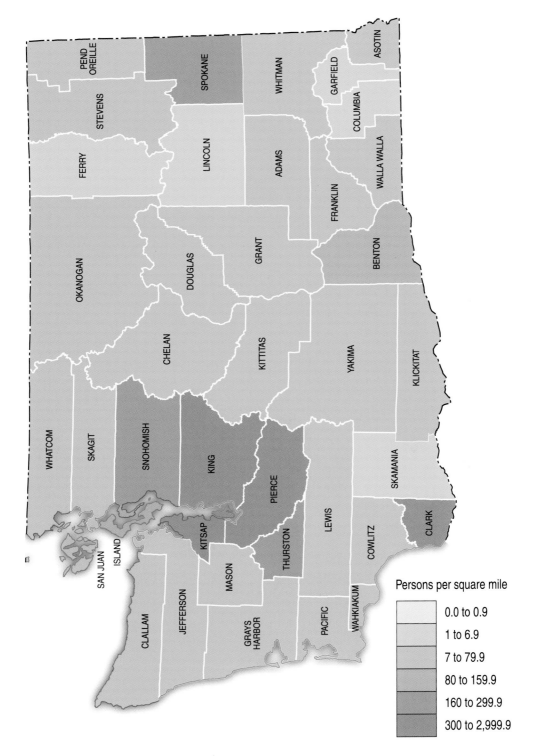

PEND OREILLE

ASOTIN

SPOKANE

WHITMAN

GARFIELD

STEVENS

COLUMBIA

FERRY

LINCOLN

ADAMS

WALLA WALLA

FRANKLIN

OKANOGAN

DOUGLAS

GRANT

BENTON

CHELAN

KITTITAS

YAKIMA

KLICKITAT

WHATCOM

SKAGIT

SNOHOMISH

KING

PIERCE

SKAMANIA

KITSAP

CLARK

SAN JUAN

ISLAND

THURSTON

LEWIS

COWLITZ

MASON

CLALLAM

JEFFERSON

GRAYS HARBOR

PACIFIC

WAHKIAKUM

Persons per square mile

0.0 to 0.9

1 to 6.9

7 to 79.9

80 to 159.9

160 to 299.9

300 to 2,999.9

BIG CITY, SMALL TOWN, COUNTRY

Washington is unbalanced. Three-fourths of the people live in less than one-third of the state, the Puget Sound Lowland. The densest concentration of people is in the megalopolis, or supercity, that stretches 87 miles from Everett to Olympia. It includes Seattle and Tacoma, the state's largest and third-largest cities.

Just as Washington's east side and west side sometimes seem to be two different states, its cities and small towns sometimes seem like two different worlds. Outside of the megalopolis, Washington is very much a western state. Country music plays at truck stops. Boots are for everyday wear, not just for weekend hiking trips. "I laugh sometimes when I see people from Seattle come up here to camp," said a native of Skykomish, in the Cascades. "They've got fancy parkas and backpacks—six, seven hundred dollars' worth of gear to do things that my brothers and I used to do in old sneakers and sweatshirts."

Still, country life is changing in Washington, as it is everywhere. Even the most rural communities are part of the larger world, linked by television, the Internet, and highways. "I can't wait until I'm old enough to move away from this town," declared a thirteen-year-old girl from Goldendale, near Mount Adams. "It has a great view of the mountain, but how many times can you look at a mountain?"

Some small communities are getting new residents—people who are leaving the big cities for a more relaxed, uncrowded way of life. "Now I can only spend about one week a month there," said Seattleite Gary Banasek, who is building a house near North Cove on the Olympic Peninsula. "But if things go right at my job, I'd like to live in the country full-time and do my work by computer."

As Washington's economy shifts from resource-based industries to services and trade, many small towns are facing economic disaster. Some have turned to tourism to stay alive. Leavenworth led the way. In the 1960s this little mountain community was on the verge of becoming a ghost town. Citizens rebuilt the town, turning it into a reproduction of a traditional village in Bavaria, in southern Germany. Today, its shops and resorts draw many visitors, with the festival of Christmas lights being the high point of the year. "Sure, the German thing is a gimmick," admitted one local teenager. "But it worked. And it's kind of fun."

Leavenworth attracts many visitors during the holidays.

Washington offers a world of possibilities for the outdoors enthusiast. Many Washingtonians spend as much time as they can hiking, camping, sailing, kayaking, scuba diving, mountain or rock climbing, skiing, snowboarding, and snowmobiling. Every year hundreds participate in the 200-mile Seattle to Portland Bicycle Classic. One popular pastime is traveling among the San Juan Islands by ferryboat, with a bicycle or kayak for up-close exploration.

Those who enjoy the outdoors find many thrilling activities in Washington.

"When people here ask what you do, they don't want to know about your job," said a twenty-four-year-old New York City woman who recently moved to Seattle. "They want to know what sports you're into. My first week on the job, someone said to me, 'Bring your skis to the office on Friday, and we'll go skiing after work.' Skis? I was embarrassed to tell them I never go outside except to walk my dog. There are people here who don't even have furniture, but they have sport utility vehicles loaded with kayaks and bikes and tents. I guess if I'm going to fit in here, I'd better learn to love the great outdoors."

Washington is also famous for its arts. One of the state's best-known artists is Dale Chihuly, whose brilliantly colored glass creations are admired around the world. Crafts influenced by Native-American arts, such as

Dale Chihuly, one of Washington's best-known artists, creates stunning creations with glass.

beadwork, basketry, and wood carving, are also popular with many in Washington. Fairs all over the state display the work of painters, jewelers, woodworkers, and potters. Dozens of festivals celebrate the arts, most notably Bumbershoot, Seattle's annual arts fair, which includes dance, comedy, and theater performances.

Washington's calendar is crammed full with other fairs and festivals. Some celebrate the state's agricultural bounty by featuring apples, berries, or tulips. Eatonville's Slug Fest honors the underappreciated banana slug (a large, shell-less snail) with slug races and a slug puppet theater.

Ethnic pride is the theme of many annual events, ranging from the all-Indian rodeo in Toppenish, in central Washington, to the Black Pioneer Picnic in Roslyn, a tiny town in the Cascades that became home to three hundred African-American coal miners and their families in the 1880s. In 1997 more than 20,000 people attended a celebration of Tet, the Vietnamese New Year, held by Vietnamese students in Seattle. Quang-Trung Pham, one of the organizers, expressed the feelings of young people from many backgrounds who take part in such traditional celebrations: "This is the first time that the younger generations have taken the responsibility to organize the most important festival in Vietnamese culture. It doesn't matter where we are, be it Paris or America, it's our culture we have to preserve."

PROBLEMS AND PROMISES

"Do you know that old saying 'Be careful what you wish for'? That's what life here in Washington is like," said a woman who lives in Issaquah, east of Seattle. "I grew up not far from here, and it was all farms. There was only one place to shop. It seemed like a big hassle to go anywhere. You knew all your neighbors, and it was boring. Now Seattle's practically on our doorstep, and I don't know if I like it."

Many Washingtonians feel the same way. Their state is changing rapidly—but is it changing for the better or the worse? Seattle is a city trying to keep its balance in a whirlwind of growth that threatens to knock it off its feet. "When we moved here in the seventies," said one resident, "I thought we had discovered the last perfect place—a wonderful city with no problems. Now we have litter, graffiti, gangs. . . . And don't even get me started about the traffic!"

For some Washingtonians Seattle sometimes seems to get too much attention. "I get tired of the way people in other parts of the country automatically think 'Seattle' when they think of Washington," said Carl Mendes. He lives in Vancouver, a city on the Columbia River directly across from Portland, Oregon. "Seattle doesn't really have much to do with my life," he continued. "Vancouver's a better place to live—close to recreation, but without the hassles of Seattle, and you can afford to buy a house here. As far as bigger cities go, I spend a lot more time in Portland."

To many people Washington is proof that states can grow and change without losing the qualities that make them special. Washington still offers residents and visitors remarkable scenery, a rich and varied cultural life, and as many recreational opportunities as any place in the world. Norman Rice, the mayor of Seattle from 1990 to 1997, summed up the challenges facing his city and state this way: "We've grown, we will continue to grow, and as we grow we will learn together. Washington can be the place that people look to when they want to see how to make the future work."

Chapter Four

Running Washington

Like other states and the United States as a whole, Washington has a constitution that allows people to elect its government officials. The state constitution also tells Washingtonians how they can create laws, settle disagreements, and make decisions about their state. The constitution dates from 1889, but it moves forward with the times. Citizens can vote to change or expand it.

INSIDE GOVERNMENT

Washington's government operates from offices in Olympia, the state capital. The government has three divisions: the executive, legislative, and judicial branches.

Executive

The executive branch is responsible for seeing that the state's laws are carried out and for determining how the state's income—raised from taxes—is spent. The governor, who is elected to a four-year term, appoints the heads of various departments and agencies, holds cabinet meetings with advisors and officials, and prepares the state budget. Other executive branch officials,

The State Capitol in Washington is a cluster of four buildings. The domed building houses the legislature.

such as the attorney general and the commissioner of public lands, oversee dozens of agencies that carry out the law in fields ranging from the environment to workplace safety.

Washington has had some notable governors. Dixy Lee Ray became the state's first woman governor. She was elected to office in 1976. A scientist who had received a doctoral degree in biology, Ray worked to improve communication and cooperation between the scientific community and the government.

In 1997 Gary Locke became the first Chinese American to be governor of any state. When Locke was sworn into office in the handsome capitol in Olympia, he noted that he was standing just a few blocks from where his grandfather worked as a servant. "One hundred years to travel one mile," he said. Locke believes that education is vital to maintaining a society where opportunities are open to people of all backgrounds. Education is "like electricity," he said. "People can plug into it at any time of their lives."

The office of governor of Washington made national news in 2004, when an election that pitted the Republican Dino Rossi against the Democrat Christine Gregoire turned into one of the closest—and most controversial—elections on record. The first vote count, done by machine, proclaimed Rossi the winner. The results were so close that a recount was done, also by machine. Again Rossi was named the winner. But a second recount, done by hand, showed Gregoire won by just 129 votes. Gregoire was sworn in as governor in January 2005. Her victory was challenged in a series of court battles in the months that followed, but in the final recount, she won by 133 votes.

The close contest highlights the tension between conservative Washingtonians (who generally vote for Republican candidates) and

As Washington's first female governor, Dixy Lee Ray balanced the state budget and oversaw full funding for basic education in the state.

liberal ones (who generally support Democrats). In general, the state's politics have mirrored its geography, with conservatives east of the Cascades and in rural areas, and liberals on the west, especially in the Seattle metro area. For some time Washington has had a liberal majority, supporting Democratic candidates in presidential elections from 1996 through 2004.

State gubernatorial candidates Christine Gregoire and Dino Rossi vied in a close race in the 2004 elections.

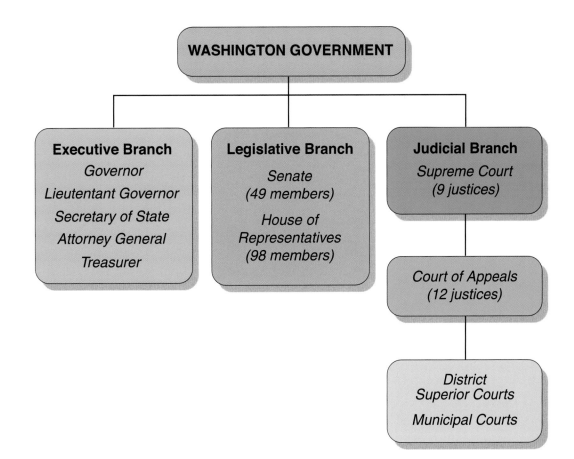

WASHINGTON GOVERNMENT

Executive Branch
Governor
Lieutentant Governor
Secretary of State
Attorney General
Treasurer

Legislative Branch
Senate
(49 members)
House of
Representatives
(98 members)

Judicial Branch
Supreme Court
(9 justices)

Court of Appeals
(12 justices)

District
Superior Courts
Municipal Courts

Legislative

The legislature is the branch of state government that makes laws. It consists of a senate and a house of representatives. Washington's voters elect forty-nine senators to four-year terms and ninety-eight representatives to two-year terms. These legislators write and vote on bills. If the governor signs a bill, it becomes law. If the governor vetoes it—decides not to sign it—it will still become law if enough members of the legislature support it.

Judicial

The judicial branch applies the law through a system of courts. The justices in municipal and district courts listen to cases ranging from parking tickets to minor property damages. Serious crimes, such as murder, are tried in superior courts. The state Supreme Court decides cases that have been appealed from lower courts. In doing so it often interprets the law in ways that affect later cases. Washington's voters elect the nine justices of the state supreme court to six-year terms.

STATE FINANCE

An elected official called a treasurer manages Washington's money, collecting the state's income and overseeing its expenses. The main source of income is taxes. Washington is one of just seven states that do not require residents to pay a state income tax on their earnings. Businesses in Washington do not pay a corporate income tax, either, although they do pay a variety of other taxes and fees.

Washingtonians pay a sales tax when they buy goods and services. In addition to a statewide sales tax, local sales taxes may appear in the final cost of goods. Counties collect property taxes on real estate within their borders. Certain products, such as gasoline and alcohol, are subject to special taxes called excises. In 2005 Washington voters rejected a move to repeal, or cancel, the tax on gasoline. As a result money from the gas tax remains available to maintain and upgrade the state's network of roads, highways, and bridges.

As in many states, Washingtonians pay a sales tax on purchases.

WASHINGTON BY COUNTY

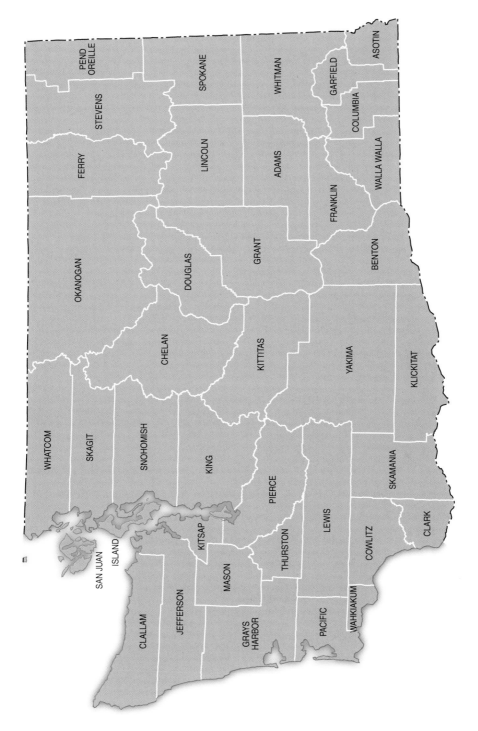

Another source of income is state-sponsored gambling through lottery games. Lottery revenue for the state has risen from about $257 million in 1989 to $458 million in 2005. To some the state-run lottery is a vital source of funding that helps support schools and other social services. Others, pointing to the fact that some people suffer from a gambling addiction that can cause serious personal and social problems, ask whether the state should be in the business of helping people gamble. Like the forty other states that sponsor lotteries, however, Washington is unlikely to reverse its position on this source of income.

POLITICAL ISSUES

Land use is one of Washington's hottest political issues, argued at every level, from the neighborhood community group to the state legislature. Pointing to the sprawl of strip malls, housing developments, and parking lots that has swallowed up hundreds of square miles near Puget Sound in recent years, some land-use planners consider urban growth a monster that must be brought under control. They want to establish urban growth limits, preserve farmland and undeveloped countryside close to cities, and develop public transportation systems instead of building even more roads and highways.

Not everyone supports these goals. "The environmentalists want us to build row houses, condos, and apartments because they take up less land," complained the owner of a Seattle-based construction company. "But most parents want their families to have a house of their own, with a yard. Shouldn't people be able to live the way they want?" Citizens in many parts of the state are getting involved in the land use debate by attending city council meetings and working to get proposals about land issues placed on ballots to allow voters to decide.

There is growing concern in Washington that too much land is being overdeveloped to support the housing market.

Crime among young people is another issue that concerns Washingtonians. People under the age of twenty-one are involved in a growing number of burglaries and other crimes, many of them related to drug and alcohol abuse. Schools, law enforcement agencies, churches, and concerned parents are looking for ways to keep kids out of trouble. "I work with young kids, ages eleven to fourteen," said Seattle's Jamile Wilde, who helps run after-school basketball games. "I don't preach at kids. They come here to play b-ball, not listen to someone like me tell them what to do. But I try to get the message across that, hey, we are all in this together, and we have no time for drugs, fighting, or racism."

Chapter Five

The Evergreen State at Work

Washington's economy is changing. In the middle of the twentieth century most Washingtonians worked in such jobs as logging or manufacturing. Now more people are employed in such service jobs as sales, banking, restaurant work, and the thriving tourist industry.

THE IMPORTANCE OF TRADE

Trade has always been important to Washington's economy. One in three working Washingtonians is directly or indirectly involved in trade. Partly because Seattle is closer to Asia than any other seaport in the mainland United States, Washington has become a leader in U.S. trade with Asia. A glimpse of Puget Sound likely reveals several huge cargo ships and barges carrying timber, paper, wheat, chemicals, computer software, or seafood to customers around the Pacific Rim in exchange for automobiles, electronic devices, clothing, and textiles.

Apple orchards in Washington provide jobs for the state's many temporary workers.

An Asian container ship unloads its cargo in Seattle.

The state exports a variety of industrial and agricultural products. Leading exports are aircraft and spacecraft; corn; soybeans; circuits and other microelectronic components; wheat; parts for balloons, aircraft, and spacecraft; data-processing equipment; processed oil; auto parts; and wood. Among Washington's top trade partners are Japan, Canada, China, South Korea, Taiwan, France, Singapore, the Netherlands, the United Kingdom, and Hong Kong.

2004 GROSS STATE PRODUCT: $253 Billion

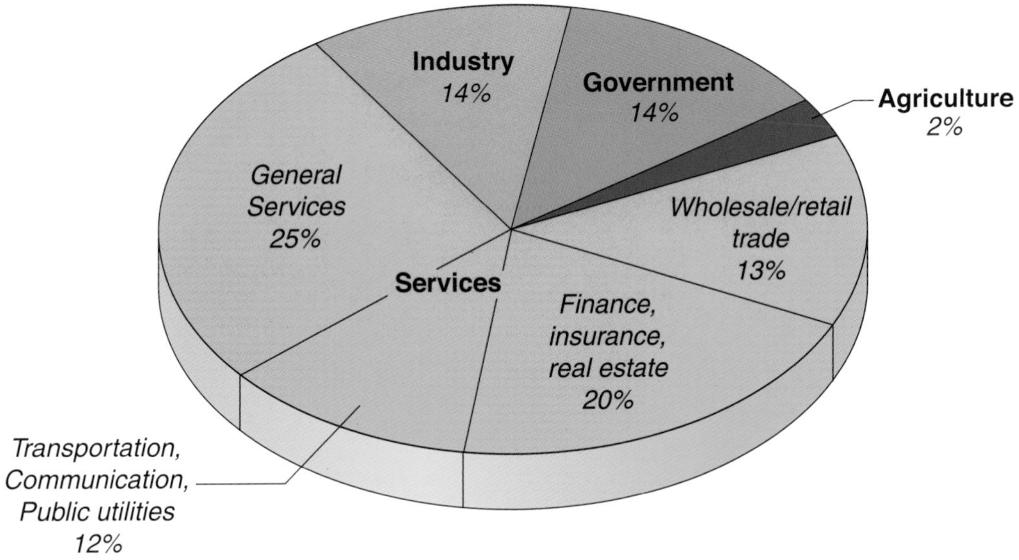

Industry 14%

Government 14%

Agriculture 2%

General Services 25%

Wholesale/retail trade 13%

Services

Finance, insurance, real estate 20%

Transportation, Communication, Public utilities 12%

INDUSTRY

The state's largest industry is producing transportation equipment. Seattle's Boeing Company is the world's leading airplane manufacturer. For years Boeing shaped Seattle's economy. When the company did well, so did the whole region—and when the company hit hard times, western Washington suffered. Between 1993 and 1995 nearly 47,000 Boeing workers lost their jobs after the company's sales fell. A turnaround came in 1996, when the company expanded and began hiring more than 50,000 new employees. Some workers remain cautious, however. "Sure, I'm glad to have a good job," said one Boeing employee. "But I knew people who got laid off in '93. It could happen to me next time." Today, however, the growing importance of other industries means that Boeing's ups and downs do not affect the region as powerfully as they once did.

Boeing's Everett plant is the largest building in the world where their jet liners are manufactured.

Other industries vital to Washington's economy are aluminum production, shipbuilding, and electronics. The Microsoft Corporation, located in Redmond, makes the world's best-selling computer software. Nintendo of America and other electronics firms are located in western Washington. The state also has a large construction industry. Rapid population and economic growth have created a great demand for new houses and other buildings. Another important employer is the U.S. military. Washington has a number of military sites, such as the Yakima Military Range and bases in Spokane and Tacoma, that contribute to local economies.

EARNING A LIVING

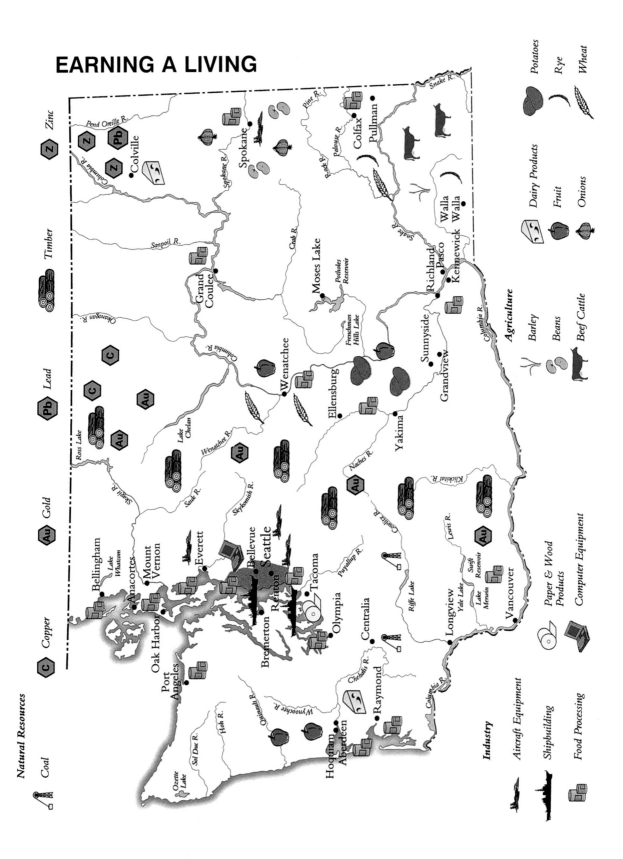

Natural Resources

Coal
Copper — C
Gold — Au
Lead — Pb
Timber
Zinc — Z

Agriculture

Potatoes
Rye
Wheat
Dairy Products
Fruit
Onions
Barley
Beans
Beef Cattle

Industry

Aircraft Equipment
Shipbuilding
Food Processing
Paper & Wood Products
Computer Equipment

Colville
Spokane
Pullman
Colfax
Walla Walla
Kennewick
Pasco
Richland
Sunnyside
Grandview
Grand Coulee
Moses Lake
Wenatchee
Ellensburg
Yakima
Bellingham
Mount Vernon
Anacortes
Everett
Seattle
Bellevue
Renton
Bremerton
Tacoma
Olympia
Centralia
Longview
Vancouver
Oak Harbor
Port Angeles
Hoquiam
Aberdeen
Raymond

Pend Oreille R.
Columbia R.
Spokane R.
Pine R.
Snake R.
Palouse R.
Rock R.
Crab R.
Sanpoil R.
Okanogan R.
Potholes Reservoir
Frenchman Hills Lake
Ross Lake
Lake Chelan
Wenatchee R.
Sauk R.
Skagit R.
Skykomish R.
Naches R.
Kittitat R.
Lewis R.
Cowlitz R.
Riffle Lake
Yale Lake
Lake Merwin
Swift Reservoir
Puyallup R.
Chehalis R.
Wynoochee R.
Quinault R.
Hoh R.
Sol Duc R.
Columbia R.
Lake Whatcom
Ozette Lake

FORESTRY, AGRICULTURE, AND FISHING

In terms of money, forestry—which includes logging, milling, and processing wood—is the state's third-largest industry. Agriculture is second largest. Key crops are apples, wheat, cherries, potatoes, raspberries, lentils, and hay.

Many farms now employ fewer people than they used to because machines perform some tasks. Still, agriculture is the state's largest employer. Traditionally, thousands of temporary or seasonal workers—many of them from Mexico—have found jobs in Washington, especially picking fruit. Some have stayed, becoming what some people called undocumented workers and others call illegal immigrants.

In May 2006 Senator Patty Murray, one of Washington's voices in the U.S. Senate, called her state's 700,000 undocumented workers the country's largest concentration of such people as a percentage of total state population. Their fate is undecided. Stricter laws against illegal immigration, passed in the wake of the 2001 terrorist attacks, may cause economic problems for Washington. Farmers might become unable to harvest their crops because of the lack of workers. Hispanic residents in Washington, like those in other parts of the country, have held demonstrations calling for reform of the immigration laws, yet other citizens, and some lawmakers, support stricter border security and controls on immigration. It is a debate that will play out in the apple orchards, asparagus fields, and vineyards of Washington State, among other places.

Large machines harvest grain on the Palouse.

YAKIMA APPLE PIE

Washington produces more apples than any other state in the country, and Washingtonians have almost as many ways of making apple pie as they have apples. This recipe for apple and cheese pie comes from an orchard owner in the Yakima Valley. She suggests using Granny Smith apples, which are juicy and not too sweet. You can make your pie crust from scratch, but "our apples are so fabulous, they make store-bought crust taste good," she boasts. Have an adult help you with this recipe.

1. Preheat the oven to 450 °F
2. Peel and core four to six apples, and cut them into thin slices. You need about 5 1/2 cups of slices for a 9-inch pie crust. Put them in a large bowl.
3. In another bowl, mix 1/2 cup sugar (either white or brown), 1/8 teaspoon salt, 1 tablespoon cornstarch, 1/4 teaspoon cinnamon, and 1/8 teaspoon nutmeg. Pour this mixture over the slices, and gently stir until the slices are coated.
4. Lay the slices in the crust in layers. The mound of slices should be lower than the edge of the crust around the outside and slightly higher in the center. Break 1 tablespoon of butter into small bits, and sprinkle them over the mound.

5. Bake the pie for 20 minutes. While the pie is baking, grate 1 cup of cheddar cheese. Take the pie out of the oven, and sprinkle the cheese over it. Set your oven to broil, and cook the pie until the cheese is melted, bubbly, and golden. Let the pie stand until it is cool enough to eat.

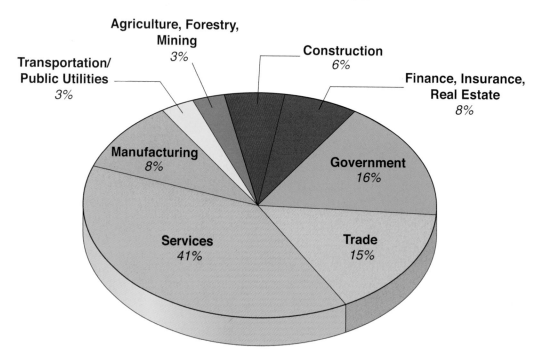

WASHINGTON WORKFORCE

Agriculture, Forestry, Mining
3%

Construction
6%

Transportation/
Public Utilities
3%

Finance, Insurance,
Real Estate
8%

Manufacturing
8%

Government
16%

Services
41%

Trade
15%

The commercial fishing industry produces about $1.6 billion in annual sales and employs some ten thousand Washingtonians. Fishing fleets harvest about three billion pounds of fish and shellfish each year from coastal and deep-sea waters. In addition, fish farms raise such fish as salmon for the market, and Washington is the nation's top producer of farmed oysters and clams.

Washingtonians recognize that traditional jobs based on natural resources do not employ as many people as they once did. As resources become scarce and machines perform more tasks, the jobs disappear. "I'm the third generation in my family to work on the water," said a commercial fisherman from Port Angeles on the Olympic Peninsula.

Seafood means big business in Washington. This vendor sells the day's catch.

"Now my son plans to study computer design. I know that's the way of the future. But," he adds, waving at the panorama of sea and sky that surrounds his boat, "it's hard to imagine him spending his life indoors."

Faced with a changing economy, some Washingtonians have found new ways to make a living on the land they love. One family owned a cattle ranch in the Methow Valley, a stunning sliver of pasture tucked into the gray crags of the North Cascades. No longer able to make money from the ranch, they risked losing their land. Then they decided to turn it into a resort for campers. "We built old-style bunkhouses, very simple," said the proud owner. "We did most of the work ourselves. Then we just started advertising. We raise llamas as pack animals for backpacking trips into the mountains, we have horseback-riding camps for kids in the summer, and in the winter we have people who come here for the cross-country skiing. We're not making a fortune, but we're getting by."

Chapter Six

Washington Road Trip

There's a lot to see and do in the Evergreen State. Washington has three national parks, three national recreation areas, six national forests, twenty-six wilderness areas, and more than one hundred state parks, as well as one of America's most dynamic and exciting cities. Pack your bag—don't forget your rain gear—and get started.

SEATTLE

Begin your tour on top of the Space Needle, the 605-foot tower that was built for the 1962 world's fair. Resembling a spaceship perched on a pole, the Space Needle is the most distinctive feature of Seattle's skyline, visible from many parts of the city. Have a meal in the rotating restaurant on top—every hour it spins through a complete circle. Then go out to the observation deck and enjoy the glorious view of the Olympic Mountains and Puget Sound in the west, the Cascades in the east, and Seattle spread out at your feet. Next to the Needle is the Experience Music Project, a museum with a wild, colorful design. Near the base of the Needle you can catch the monorail. Also built for the fair, the monorail is a train

Natural wonders such as old-growth forests draw many tourists to Washington.

Seattle's Space Needle makes for a dramatic sight along the city's skyline.

that runs on a single track raised above the ground. It will whisk you downtown for more exploring.

Some Seattle landmarks are not to be missed. Pike Place Market, which opened in 1907 as a market for Italian immigrant farmers, covers several blocks and contains dozens of stores that sell everything from jewel-bright fresh fruit to fragrant beeswax candles to locally made handicrafts. Watch out when you pass one of the fish stalls, though—the workers there are famous for throwing fish through the air. "Never hit a customer yet!" they boast.

Rebuilt after a fire destroyed most of downtown Seattle in 1889, Pioneer Square contains many of the city's oldest buildings, as well as a giant totem pole and a statue of Chief Seattle. Here you can take a tour of Seattle's Underground, which was created during reconstruction after the fire.

A totem pole is found among the twenty city blocks that make up Pioneer Square.

To make the neighborhood's hills less steep, Seattleites raised the level of the streets by roofing over the old sidewalks and stores and building above them. Some below-street-level buildings remained in use as taverns and gambling houses until the 1930s. Today's Underground, spooky but safe, is considerably tamer than it was in former times.

A giant troll lives under Seattle's Aurora Bridge—in statue form. Posing in its lap for photographs is popular with many visitors. Not far away is another famous statue, *Waiting for the Interurban*. It depicts a group of life-size people waiting to catch a trolley. Often the statues wear hats, clothes, or costumes arranged by prankish local residents.

Seattle has a number of excellent museums, but if you can see only one, make it the Thomas Burke Memorial Washington State Museum on the University of Washington campus. It is famous for its exhibits of the Northwest's natural wonders, including dinosaur bones, and of Native American art and culture. You can also experience Indian culture at the Tillicum Village Northwest Coast Native American Cultural Center on Blake Island, a forty-five-minute boat ride from Seattle. There, Indians perform traditional dances, serve salmon baked in the Native-American style, and maintain a museum.

You could spend many days absorbing all that Seattle has to offer, but the rest of the state is waiting. Head north along the sound. A bridge will take you to Whidbey Island, and from there you can take a ferry to the other San Juan Islands, Washington's watery playground. The islands are a world of villages and inns, salt breezes, seafood dinners, and blue horizons. Visit San Juan Island National Historical Park near the town of Friday Harbor. You'll see the remains of English and American forts from the 1850s, when the two nations nearly went to war after an American farmer shot a British-owned pig.

A day sail among the San Juan Islands is a perfect opportunity to whale watch.

TO THE EAST SIDE

The most dramatic way to go from western Washington to eastern Washington is over the North Cascades Highway. It starts in the flat, tranquil Skagit Valley, which is a red and yellow blaze of tulip blossoms in the spring. Then it winds up and up into North Cascades National Park, in which you'll be surrounded by white glaciers, steep gray stone pinnacles, and one of the largest wilderness areas in the nation, Green Mountain Meadow. Hours later, after a long descent through forested valleys, you'll be on the other side of the mountains.

Wildflowers bloom near snowcapped mountains in North Cascades National Park.

Head south to Lake Chelan, a deep, narrow, 55-mile-long gash in the mountains, carved by glaciers long ago and now full of clear, cold water. You can ride a ferry up the lake to Stehekin, an isolated, roadless community that is the starting point for backpacking adventures. Or go northeast, toward the Okanogan Highlands and the Colville Reservation. Maybe you'll catch the Omak Stampede and World Famous Suicide Race, called "the most dangerous race in the world." In a seven-decade-old tradition Native Americans on horses plunge down a steep cliff and across the Okanogan River.

Don't miss Grand Coulee Dam, the largest producer of electricity in the United States. Nearly a mile long, measuring 550 feet from bedrock to the road across its top, Grand Coulee contains enough concrete to build a 4-foot-wide sidewalk around the world—twice. "Ooh, this is the best part," says a ten-year-old visitor during the steep, scary ride in a glass elevator down

Hydroelectric power is generated by twenty-four generators at the Grand Coulee Dam.

into the dam to view the giant turbines and other machinery housed there. Nearby is Sun Lakes State Park, where you can see a geological marvel called Dry Falls. Its cliffs, 3.5 miles wide and 400 feet high, were the site of the world's largest waterfall several thousand years ago, before the Columbia River changed its course.

In Spokane is the Northwest Museum of Arts & Culture, the home of the Eastern Washington State Historical Society. Its displays tell the story of the inland empire, from dinosaur days to the railroad boom. Some exhibits feature items made by Indians from Alaska to Argentina. The Indians of the Columbia Plateau are represented by collections of clothing, beaded skin bags, and baskets made of woven corn husks.

Leaving Spokane, travel southwest through the Palouse. The wind bends the grain and stirs the dust of empty fields, the sky looks very large above the endless rolling hills, and you can go for miles and miles without seeing another car. Along Washington's southern border you'll rejoin the Columbia River, and gradually the mountains will rise over the western horizon. As you approach Mount Adams, stop at the Maryhill Museum of Art, a mansion high on a hill overlooking the river. Peacocks roam the grounds of the museum, which contains collections of unusual chessboards, French sculptures, and items once owned by the royal family of Romania. Not far from the museum is a concrete replica of Stonehenge, England's prehistoric stone monument. The replica is a memorial to local soldiers who died in World War I.

If you're in the nearby town of Goldendale when dusk falls, visit the Goldendale Observatory. It has a 24-inch telescope, one of the largest in the country open for public viewing. At night the astronomers turn the telescope to different patches of sky—the moon, the rings of Saturn, or a distant galaxy.

PLACES TO SEE

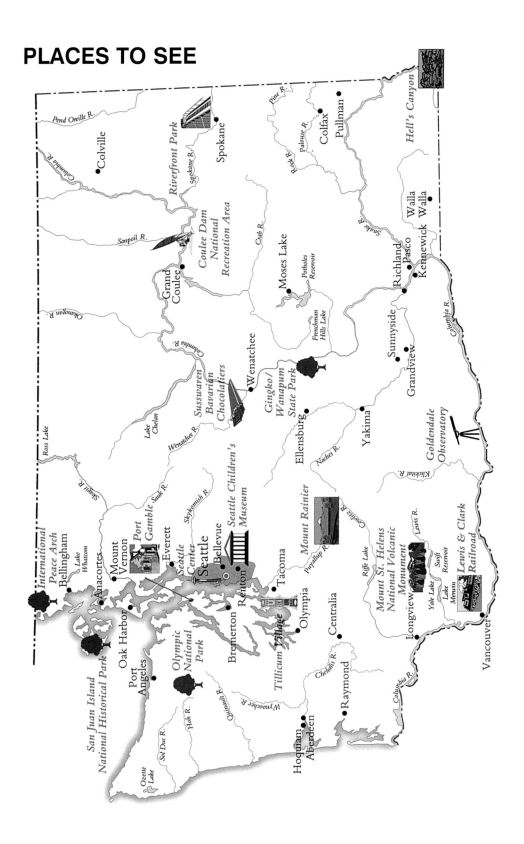

Pend Oreille R.

Colville

Columbia R.

Spokane R.

Riverfront Park

Spokane

Pine R.

Palouse R.

Rock R.

Colfax

Pullman

Hell's Canyon

Sanpoil R.

Coulee Dam National Recreation Area

Crab R.

Moses Lake

Potholes Reservoir

Walla Walla

Snake R.

Richland

Pasco

Kennewick

Grand Coulee

Okanogan R.

Columbia R.

Freenchman Hills Lake

Columbia R.

Sunnyside

Grandview

Wenatchee

Sussvaren Bavarian Chocolatiers

Gingko/ Wanapum State Park

Ross Lake

Wenatchee R.

Lake Chelan

Ellensburg

Naches R.

Yakima

Goldendale Observatory

Klickitat R.

Skagit R.

Seattle Children's Museum

Skykomish R.

Sauk R.

Mount Rainier

Cowlitz R.

Lewis R.

Lewis & Clark Railroad

International Peace Arch

Bellingham

Lake Whatcom

Mount Vernon

Port Gamble

Everett

Seattle Center

Seattle

Bellevue

Tacoma

Puyallup R.

Riffe Lake

Mount St. Helens National Volcanic Monument

Swift Reservoir

Yale Lake

Lake Merwin

Oak Harbor

Anacortes

Port Angeles

Olympic National Park

Bremerton

Renton

Olympia

Centralia

Longview

Vancouver

Tillicum Village

San Juan Island National Historical Park

Sol Duc R.

Hoh R.

Quinault R.

Wynoochee R.

Chehalis R.

Raymond

Ozette Lake

Hoquiam

Aberdeen

Columbia R.

INTO THE MOUNTAINS

Heading northwest, you'll want to stop in Mount Rainier National Park as you cross the Cascades again. The park contains the Grove of the Patriarchs, a cluster of some of the largest and oldest trees in the state. It also contains Paradise, a huge, old-fashioned lodge high on the mountain's flank. Rainier's smooth, ice-capped dome is even more impressive up close than on a distant skyline, but sometimes it's the small things that count. "I come here every spring for the wildflowers," said seventy-six-year-old Eileen Dudley Wells of Tacoma. "There are more than three hundred different kinds of wildflowers growing around this mountain, and each one is beautiful. The mountains wouldn't be complete without them. I want to see every one of 'em before I die."

Mount Saint Helens National Volcanic Monument will stun you with mile upon mile of fallen trees, blasted by the 1980 eruption. You can climb to an overlook above Spirit Lake, once a Pacific Northwest showplace, now full of logs and mud. If you're a good hiker, you can climb a trail to the volcano's rim and peek into the steaming depths. If that doesn't sound too inviting, several well-designed visitors' centers offer dramatic films of the eruption and information about how nature is returning life to the devastated landscape.

No visit to Washington is complete without a view of majestic Mount Rainier.

ROADSIDE ODDITIES

Washington's highways and byways sometimes offer surprises. Take Bickleton, a small town near the Columbia River, in central Washington. To encourage endangered bluebirds to nest and raise families, the people of Bickleton have filled their town with a multitude of specially designed nest boxes. Or Raymond, a town of three thousand people, in the southwest, which has lined the highway through town with life-size metal sculptures of deer, birds, horses and wagons, and people in pioneer-style clothing.

Some communities express themselves through murals. Wall paintings on the sides of stores and businesses depict events in the history of Long Beach, and outdoor murals display scenes from the early days in Centralia, a city founded in 1875 by the black pioneer George Washington. Kalama, founded in the 1840s and named after a Hawaiian man who married a local Indian woman, has a totem pole thought to be the world's tallest. Made from a single tree, it is 140 feet high. "You really need to keep your eyes open around here," said one visitor from Pennsylvania. "You never know what's coming up."

West of the mountains, drop in on Oysterville. This tiny town on the Long Beach Peninsula in southwest Washington came into being during the mid-1800s, when oysters were plentiful in the local waters. Tradition says that the oyster-fishing industry was so prosperous that for a few years, local communities had more gold than any place on the

TEN LARGEST CITIES

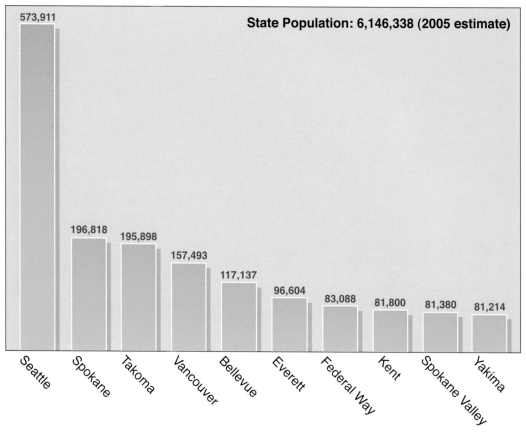

State Population: 6,146,338 (2005 estimate)

- Seattle: 573,911
- Spokane: 196,818
- Takoma: 195,898
- Vancouver: 157,493
- Bellevue: 117,137
- Everett: 96,604
- Federal Way: 83,088
- Kent: 81,800
- Spokane Valley: 81,380
- Yakima: 81,214

West Coast except San Francisco. Today it's a quiet backwater, perfect for walking on the beach and bird-watching.

Farther north you can explore the Olympic Peninsula. The beaches are magnificent, but this coast is not for swimming—perils include logs tossed in the waves, cold temperatures, and undertows. A trip to Olympic National Park should include a hike through the Hoh Rain Forest, which ten-year-old Nathan, a visitor from California, called "the greenest place on Earth." This wet, lush wilderness has enormous trees, as well as the Hall of Mosses, a photographer's favorite because of its many shades of green. Continuing north and east around the peninsula, get a different view of the park from Hurricane Ridge, more than 5,200 feet above sea level. From there you'll see a panorama of peaks, with Mount Olympus in the center.

Descending from the Olympics, make your way eastward, past fishing towns, campgrounds, and clear-cuts, to a ferry port on the Kitsap Peninsula. Climb aboard the ferry, settle into a seat, and look east. You're headed back to where your trip began. If you're lucky, your first glimpse of Seattle will come just as night falls, and the city will be a blaze of lights reflected in the sound, with the luminous Space Needle floating above it all.

Downtown Seattle lights up as evening approaches.

THE FLAG: The flag, adopted in 1923, displays the state seal on a dark green background, which symbolizes the state's forests. It was readopted in 1967, when a new portrait of George Washington was chosen for the seal.

THE SEAL: The seal is a portrait of George Washington painted by Gilbert Stuart. Around the portrait are the words "The Seal of the State of Washington 1889." The first seal, adopted in 1889, used a likeness of Washington from a postage stamp. The Gilbert Stuart portrait replaced that likeness in 1967.

State Survey

Statehood: November 11, 1889

Origin of Name: Named after the first U.S. president, George Washington

Nicknames: The Evergreen State, the Chinook State

Capital: Olympia

Motto: Al-ki (Chinook trade jargon word for "bye and bye")

Bird: Willow goldfinch

Flower: Coast rhododendron

Tree: Western hemlock

Fish: Steelhead trout

Gem: Petrified wood

Colors: Green and gold

Dance: Square dance

Goldfinch

Rhododendron

WASHINGTON, MY HOME

On March 19, 1959, at a Washington's birthday observance in the state senate, a piano was wheeled out onto the chamber floor, and "Washington, My Home" was performed by a trio, including the composer, Helen Davis. The rendition brought down the house, and it was unanimously adopted as the official state song then and there.

Helen Davis

GEOGRAPHY

Highest Point: 14,410 feet above sea level, at Mount Rainier

Lowest Point: sea level, at the Pacific Ocean

Area: 71,303 square miles

Greatest Distance North to South: 239 miles

Greatest Distance East to West: 370 miles

Bordering States: Idaho to the east, Oregon to the south

Hottest Recorded Temperature: 118 °F at Ice Harbor Dam on August 5, 1961

Coldest Recorded Temperature: 48 °F at Mazama and Winthrop on December 30, 1968

Average Annual Precipitation: 38 inches

Major Rivers: Columbia, Cowlitz, Lewis, Okanogan, Pend Oreille, Sanpoil, Skagit, Skykomish, Snake, Spokane, Yakima

Major Lakes: Chelan, Cle Elum, Crescent, Cushman, Kachess, Moses, Ozette, Quinault, Franklin D. Roosevelt, Sammamish, Soap, Washington, Wenatchee, Whatcom

Trees: alder, aspen, cottonwood, Douglas fir, lodgepole pine, maple, ponderosa pine, Sitka spruce, western hemlock, western larch, western red cedar

Wild Plants: brown-eyed Susan, everlasting lily, fern, Flett's violet, goldenrod, heather, lace, lupine, monkey flower, moss, mountain phlox, Oregon grape, piper bluebell, sagebrush, sea rose, shooting star, sunflower, western rhododendron, wild onion

Animals: badger, beaver, bobcat, clam, cougar, crab, deer, flying squirrel, gopher, marmot, marten, mink, mountain goat, muskrat, seal, sea lion

Badger

Birds: bald eagle, cormorant, duck, falcon, golden eagle, goldfinch, goose, gull, hawk, oystercatcher, pelican, pheasant, quail, ruffed grouse, sage grouse, sandpiper, shrike, swan, tern, turkey vulture, turnstone, vireo, waxwing, western lark

Fish: albacore tuna, cod, cutthroat trout, flounder, grayling, halibut, rainbow trout, salmon, steelhead trout, sturgeon, whitefish

Endangered Animals: black right whale, blue whale, brown pelican, Columbia white-tailed deer, fin whale, gray wolf, humpback whale, leatherback sea turtle, pygmy rabbit, sei whale, sperm whale

Brown pelican

Endangered Plants: Bradshaw's desert-parsley, showy stickseed, Wenatchee Mountains checkermallow

TIMELINE

Washington History

1700s Region inhabited by many tribes, including Nez Perce, Spokane, Yakima, Cayuse, Walla Walla, Nooksack, Chinook, Nisqually, and Quinault.

1775 Spanish explorers Bruno de Heceta and Juan Francisco de la Bodega y Quadra land near Point Grenville.

1778 English explorer James Cook sails along coast of Washington.

1791 Spanish establish colony on Neah Bay.

1792 American Robert Gray discovers mouth of Columbia River; British captain George Vancouver maps the Washington coast and Puget Sound.

1805 Lewis and Clark follow Columbia River to Pacific Ocean.

1811 Fort Okanogan becomes first American settlement in Washington.

1818 United States and Great Britain agree to jointly occupy Oregon region.

1825 Hudson's Bay Company builds Fort Vancouver.

1836 Mission founded at Waiilatpu, near Walla Walla.

1840s First major wave of settlers arrive.

1846 Oregon Treaty between Britain and the United States establishes 49th parallel as border between Washington and Canada; Olympia founded.

1847 Cayuse War breaks out between Cayuse Indians and settlers.

1848 Oregon Territory, which includes Washington, is created.

1851 Seattle is founded.

1853 Washington Territory created by Congress; capital established at Olympia.

1855 Discovery of gold in northeastern Washington brings rush of settlers and sparks four years of warfare between settlers and Indians.

1863 Establishment of Idaho Territory gives Washington its present border.

1883 Northern Pacific Railway's cross-country line reaches Puget Sound.

1889 Washington becomes forty-second state.

1910 Washington becomes fifth state to extend voting rights to women.

1928 Capitol in Olympia is completed.

1941 Grand Coulee Dam is completed.

1962 World's fair is held in Seattle.

1976 Dixy Lee Ray is elected state's first woman governor.

1979 U.S. Supreme Court upholds Indians' right to catch half the salmon returning to the waters where they traditionally fished.

1980 Mount Saint Helens erupts, killing fifty-seven people and causing billions of dollars in damage.

1996 Remains of prehistoric Kennewick Man found on banks of Columbia River.

2004 Renewed volcanic activity at Mount Saint Helens.

ECONOMY

Agricultural Products: apples, beef cattle, flower bulbs, milk, timber, wheat

Timber

Manufactured Products: airplanes, chemicals, computer equipment, food products, paper products, ships

Natural Resources: clay, coal, copper, gold, lead, limestone, silver, talc, tungsten, zinc

Business and Trade: banking, health care, transportation, utilities, wholesale and retail trade

CALENDAR OF CELEBRATIONS

Whale Fest Prepare to be awed by the sheer power of the great mammals of the sea. During the spring more than 20,000 gray whales migrate north. Daily whale-watch excursions leave from Westport.

Daffodil Festival Imagine the sight and smell of all those spring flowers. Tacoma celebrates the arrival of spring with one of the largest flower festivals in the country. Parades of floats, bands, drill teams, and mounted units keep the energy running high during this three-week April event.

Puyallup Spring Fair This April celebration at the fairgrounds in Puyallup features exhibits, food, entertainment, animals, and carnival rides.

Rainfest Rain is plentiful in parts of Washington, so residents make the best of it by celebrating instead of complaining. Each April, Forks celebrates the wet weather with umbrella decorating, a bicycle rodeo, an art show, and a children's carnival.

Puyallup Spring Fair

Holland Days Enjoy a taste of Dutch heritage at this May festival in Lynden, the state's largest Dutch settlement. Learn abut Dutch customs, including street scrubbing and klompen dancing, and participate in games and wooden-shoe races.

Walla Walla Balloon Stampede Each May in Walla Walla you can watch a fleet of hot-air balloons rise slowly into the sky and sky-divers jump from planes. On the ground you can enjoy a barbecue and an arts and crafts show.

Ski to Sea Race Skiers, runners, canoeists, bicyclists, and sailors compete in this 85-mile relay race from Mount Baker to Bellingham Bay in May. But you don't have to compete to get in on the fun. Bellingham welcomes the participants and fans with parades, carnival rides, games, and street fairs.

Yakima Air Fair Are you fascinated by flight? Then be sure to visit the Yakima Air Fair in June. See military, antique, warbird, and commercial aircraft. Watch fliers perform precision military aerobatics. At night keep looking to the sky for fireworks.

Lummi Stommish This June water carnival in Bellingham features canoe races, arts and crafts, salmon bakes, and Native-American dancing.

Loggerodeo If it's July, it's time for the town of Sedro-Woolley to celebrate its logging heritage with tree felling, tree climbing, and other logging competitions.

Walla Walla Balloon Stampede

Toppenish Pow Wow and Rodeo At this July festival of Indian culture in Toppenish, you can eat authentic Yakima foods, watch traditional dances and games, and enjoy a carnival, a rodeo, and a parade.

Pacific Northwest Scottish Highland Games Traditional Scottish dancers and pipe bands compete in this annual July event in Enumclaw. Food and games add to the fun.

Omak Stampede and World Famous Suicide Race In August on the Colville Reservation, you can thrill to a rodeo and the famous "suicide" ride on horseback down a cliff and across the Okanogan River.

International Kite Festival On Long Beach Peninsula each August you can observe different kinds of kite events, from handcrafted kites to stunt kites to lighted night flying. You can also get some pointers on flying your own kite and enjoy a fireworks display.

Makah Days This August festival in Neah Bay marks the day in 1913 when the American flag first flew over the Makah Reservation. The celebration includes an arts and crafts fair, canoe races, games, dancing, a parade, fireworks, and a salmon bake.

Wooden Boat Festival Wooden boatbuilding and restoration may be a dying art, but you won't think so if you come to this autumn festival in Port Townsend. You can see how the boats have changed over the years as hundreds of classic wooden boats come to port.

Omak Stampede and World Famous Suicide Race

Christmas Lighting Festival Get into the holiday spirit with the lights and decorations in Leavenworth, which is modeled after a Bavarian village. You'll also want to bundle up for an old-fashioned sleigh ride.

Yule Fest Poulsbo celebrates its Norwegian heritage with traditional foods, folk dances, games, and other celebrations of the Christmas season, including Santa's arrival by boat.

STATE STARS

William Edward Boeing (1881–1956), born in Detroit, was a pioneer in the aerospace industry. After studying at Yale University, he joined his father's lumber business in Seattle. In 1916 he founded the Pacific Aero Products Company, which became the Boeing Airplane Company, the world's largest airplane manufacturer. In 1927 he also founded Boeing Air Transport, which later became United Airlines.

Robert William (Bobby) Brown (1924–   ), born in Seattle, is both a baseball player and a cardiologist. He played third base for the New York Yankees and competed in four World Series in the late 1940s and early 1950s. He was also president of the American League from 1984 to 1994.

JoAnne Gunderson Carner (1939–   ), a professional golfer, was born in Kirkland. Carner was the U.S. Women's Amateur champion five times before turning professional in 1970. One of the leading money winners of the Ladies Professional Golf Association, she won more than forty tournaments and was named Player of the Year three times.

Carol Channing (1921–   ), an actress and singer, was born in Seattle. She is best known for her musical roles on Broadway. Channing won a 1964 Tony Award for her starring role in *Hello, Dolly!*, a role she has performed more than 4,500 times on Broadway as well as all over the world.

Carol Channing

Bing Crosby (1903–1977) born in Tacoma, was a popular singer and actor from the 1930s until his death. He made more than 1,500 recordings, including the best-selling "White Christmas." In 1944 he won the best actor Academy Award for the movie *Going My Way*.

Merce Cunningham (1919–   ) has choreographed pieces for his own dance company and for many other modern and classical dance companies around the world. He is known for his innovative techniques and has won numerous awards, including the National Medal of Arts in 1990. Cunningham was born in Centralia, began dancing at a young age, and received additional formal dance training in Seattle.

William O. Douglas (1898–1980) was a Supreme Court justice from 1939 to 1975. He was born in Minnesota and grew up in Washington. He is best remembered for his support of civil rights, conservation, and civil liberties and for his opposition to press censorship. His writings include *A Wilderness Bill of Rights* and *Of Men and Mountains*.

Tom Foley (1923–   ), who was born in Spokane, served as Speaker of the House of Representatives from 1989 to 1994. He was first elected to Congress as a Democrat in 1964. He was known for his ability to get House members to work together.

Bill Gates (1955–   ), a leader in the computer industry, was born in Seattle. He is one of the richest and most influential people in the world. With a friend, Paul Allen, he founded Microsoft, the first microcomputer software company. His company developed the Windows operating system, which is used in most personal computers. In the 1990s his company also entered the online services market.

Bill Gates

Jimi Hendrix (1942–1970), a rock guitarist, singer, and composer, was born in Seattle. Combining rock and blues with a powerful guitar style, he became a legendary performer. Onstage, he was wild and intense and one of rock's best guitarists. His songs include "Purple Haze" and "Fire."

Henry "Scoop" Jackson (1912–1983), born in Everett, was a Democratic senator from Washington for thirty years, beginning in 1953. In 1972 and 1976 he campaigned unsuccessfully for the Democratic nomination for president. He was a liberal in social matters, supporting civil rights and the environment. However, he was more conservative in foreign affairs and supported a strong national defense.

Robert Joffrey (1930–1988), born in Seattle, was a modern dance choreographer and the founder of the Joffrey Ballet. He served as artistic director of this New York City dance company until his death. The company is known for its wide range of dance styles.

Chief Joseph (1840–1904) was a chief of the Nez Perce Nation, which once occupied much of the region where Washington, Oregon, and Idaho meet. When war broke out between U.S. settlers and the Nez Perce in 1877, Chief Joseph defeated the larger U.S. forces in several battles before leading his people over rough terrain toward Canada. Federal troops overcame him 40 miles from the border. Because his people were starving and most of his warriors were dead or wounded, he surrendered with the words, "I will fight no more forever." He died on the Colville Reservation in Washington.

Jimi Hendrix

Gary Larson (1950–   ), a cartoonist, was born in Tacoma. His comic strip, *The Far Side*, which features visual puns and talking animals, has been one of the most popular cartoons of recent decades.

Mary McCarthy (1912–1989), born in Seattle, was a novelist and short story writer. Her most famous work is *The Group*, a novel that follows the lives of eight graduates of Vassar College, which McCarthy attended. McCarthy was well-known for satirizing marriage and the role of women in America. She also wrote political and travel essays, book reviews, and theater criticism.

John McLoughlin (1784–1857) was born in Quebec and briefly studied medicine before he joined the British Hudson's Bay Company and traveled to the Pacific Northwest. He built Fort Vancouver, now in Vancouver, Washington. His friendly policies toward American settlers angered his Hudson's Bay bosses.

Edward R. Murrow (1908–1965) was a pioneer in radio and television journalism. Born in North Carolina, he graduated from Washington State College. His popular *Hear It Now* CBS radio show became a television show, *See It Now*, which he hosted from 1951 to 1958. His most famous show aired in March 1954, when he attacked Senator Joseph McCarthy's communist witch hunt. Murrow's *Person to Person* show aired from 1953 to 1969. After leaving CBS, he headed the United States Information Agency.

Edward R. Murrow

Theodore Roethke (1908–1963), a distinguished poet, taught at the University of Washington from 1947 to 1963. He won a Pulitzer Prize in poetry for *The Waking* and the National Book Award for the collection *Words for the Wind*. He was known for his poetic exploration of human psychology.

Smohalla (c. 1815–1907), a member of the Wanapum Indians of the Columbia River Valley, was a teacher and prophet. His Dreamer Cult dancers urged Indians to return to traditional ways of life. He claimed that through visions and dance, they could restore the land to the Indians and bring back traditional lifeways. He greatly influenced the Indian efforts to resist white settlement in the region.

George Vancouver (1757–1798) was an English navigator and explorer who surveyed the west coast of North America. Between 1791 and 1794 he explored Puget Sound. He was the first explorer to survey Vancouver Island, which was named for him.

Marcus Whitman (1802–1847), a doctor and missionary, was born in Rushville, New York. He and his wife, Narcissa, founded a mission among the Cayuse Indians at Waiilatpu, near present-day Walla Walla, that became an important stopping place for settlers. The Cayuse turned on Whitman when they thought he was practicing sorcery, because he was immune to the diseases brought by the white man that were threatening the Cayuse. He and twelve others were killed by the Cayuse.

Theodore Roethke

Minoru Yamasaki (1912–1986), born in Seattle, was a noted architect. His huge, dramatic buildings, with Gothic arches and windows, include the St. Louis, Missouri, airport, the building housing the Woodrow Wilson School of Public and International Affairs in Princeton, New Jersey, and the World Trade Center in New York City.

TOUR THE STATE

Aberdeen Museum of History (Aberdeen) This museum uses period furnishing to re-create living conditions from the town's pioneer days in the 1880s. You can tour a home, a general store, a one-room school, a blacksmith shop, and a church. Among the museum's highlights is its collection of antique firefighting equipment.

Grays Harbor Historical Seaport (Aberdeen) This museum and interpretive center features exhibits on the history of maritime exploration in the Pacific Northwest, including a replica of Robert Gray's ship, on which he sailed along the Northwest Coast.

Fairhaven District (Bellingham) Planners for this area, built in the late 1800s, hoped that it would become a center of commerce, the "Chicago of the Northwest." Today the historic buildings house restaurants and theaters. Take a walking tour to appreciate the past.

Bremerton Naval Museum (Bremerton) You'll receive a quick lesson in naval history by visiting this museum's displays of ship models, naval weapons and equipment, and photographs. Take a look at one of the world's oldest guns, a wooden device from China. You can also tour a naval graveyard, which houses retired submarines, cruisers, and the battleship *Missouri*.

Turnbull National Wildlife Refuge (Cheney) This refuge is home to more than two hundred species of bird, along with deer, elk, coyote, beaver, mink, and other small animals. It's a great place to enjoy a hike or picnic.

Keller Historical Park (Colville) Step into the early twentieth century as you tour Colville's first schoolhouse, a farmstead cabin, a trapper's cabin, a sawmill, and a building housing antique farming tools. A lookout tower and museum are also part of this park.

Grand Coulee Dam (Coulee Dam) This is one of the world's largest concrete structures, and its power plants contain some of the world's largest hydroelectric generators. You can tour the dam, ride down to the power plant in a glass elevator, and enjoy a laser show during the summer.

Fort Spokane (Coulee Dam) This was one of the last nineteenth-century military outposts built to maintain peace between settlers and Native Americans. Today, four of its forty-five buildings remain, including the brick guardhouse, which is now a visitors' center and museum.

Olmstead Place State Park (Ellensburg) This turn-of-the-century farm has been converted into a living historical farm. It features eight buildings, wildlife, flowers and trees, and an interpretive trail. During the second weekend of September a threshing bee and antique farm equipment show are held. You can also watch demonstrations of blacksmithing and plowing.

Mud Mountain Dam (Enumclaw) Bring a picnic, cool off in a wading pool, or hike the nature trails near one of the world's highest earth-and rock-fill dams.

Grant County Pioneer Village and Museum (Ephrata) Visit a pioneer homestead and village with twenty buildings, including a church, schoolhouse, saloon, barbershop, jail, and firehouse. Displays feature Native American artifacts and trace the region's natural history and early development by white settlers.

Hoquiam's "Castle" (Hoquiam) The lumber tycoon Robert Lytle built this twenty-room mansion in 1897, and it still contains Victorian furnishings. A saloon has been re-created to give you a feel for the period.

Mount Rainier National Park (Packwood) Hike, fish, ski, mountain climb, picnic, camp, and explore nature at this spectacular park, which is home to mountain goat, mountain lion, bear, elk, and eagle. Mount Rainier, 14,410 feet about sea level, is the fifth-highest mountain in the lower forty-eight states and the largest volcano in the Cascade Range.

Mount St. Helens Visitors' Center (Castle Rock) This site includes a walk-through model of the Mount Saint Helens volcano, which last erupted in 2004. It also features a history of the mountain, volcano-monitoring equipment, views of the volcano, and a nature trail. Some hiking trails cut through nearby Mount Saint Helens National Volcanic Monument, which covers 110,000 acres of forestland that is renewing itself after being destroyed by the eruption. Helicopter and airplane sightseeing tours are also available from area airports.

Makah Cultural and Research Center (Neah Bay) At this museum you can learn about Northwest Indian culture. The center includes exhibits on Makah and other Northwest Coast Indians, 500-year-old artifacts, a 2,000-year-old Makah village, canoes, and a longhouse.

State Capitol (Olympia) On the grounds of this complex are beautiful Japanese cherry trees, a replica of Copenhagen's Tivoli Gardens' fountain, sunken gardens, and World War I and Vietnam memorials. The 287-foot capitol dome is one of the largest in the world.

Olympic National Park (Port Angeles) This park features a wide range of terrain, including seashores and snow-capped mountains, glaciers and rain forests. The park's rain forests are among the wettest places in the nation, receiving 135 inches of rain annually. Visitors can camp, fish, hike, or cruise on paddle-wheel boats.

Olympic National Park

Pike Place Market (Seattle) This vibrant market is the oldest continuously operating farmers' market in the United States, selling goods ranging from vegetables to antiques. It opened in 1907, and many of its original buildings have been restored.

Pike Place Market

Seattle Center (Seattle) You'll find a lot to do within the site of the 1962 world's fair. The grounds include gardens, plazas, sculptures, and fountains. Both the children's museum and the Pacific Science Center include many hands-on exhibits. Ride to the top of the 605-foot Space Needle and look out over the Puget Sound region. Then spend some time at the Fun Forest Amusement Park.

The Seattle Aquarium (Seattle) This watery exhibit features a 400,000-gallon underwater viewing center of Northwest marine life. The tide pool exhibit re-creates the state's coast, and such marine mammals as sea otters and seals swim in pools.

Boeing Field—King County International Airport (Seattle) Forty aircraft are on display at this museum of flight. Exhibits include a restored World War II Corsair, a 1929 Boeing Model 80A-1, an Apollo command module, and other recent jets.

Point Defiance Zoo & Aquarium (Tacoma) At this zoo you'll get to know the animals of the Pacific Rim, including polar bear, beluga whale, shark, sea otter, and walrus. Featured habitats include Arctic tundra, Puget Sound's rocky shores, and the tropics of the South Pacific. The North Pacific Aquarium displays the marine life of Puget Sound. The South Pacific Reef Aquarium is teeming with tropical fish and shark.

Fort Vancouver National Historic Site (Vancouver) In 1849 the first U.S. military outpost in the Northwest was founded in Vancouver. It was closed in 1860 but has been partially reconstructed and now includes a kitchen, a washhouse, a stockade wall, a bake house, a blacksmith shop, and other facilities.

In 1870 two climbers reached the summit of Mount Rainier and planted U.S. flags. This was the first recorded climb to the summit by white explorers. Neither of the flags they planted, however, had the thirty-seven stars appropriate for the time. One bore only thirteen stars, because it had to be sewn in a hurry the night before the expedition. The other was eleven years old and had only thirty-two stars.

In the early twentieth century loggers strapped 1,000-foot-long bundles of logs together with 150 tons of chain to form rafts. They floated these giant rafts from the Columbia River to San Diego.

The first city monorail service in the country began operation in Seattle in 1962. It connected downtown Seattle with the world's fair grounds.

Find Out More

Want to learn more about Washington? Check your local library or bookstore for these titles:

GENERAL STATE BOOKS

Marshall, John. *Washington: Portrait of a State*. Portland, OR: Graphic Arts Books, 2006.

Webster, Christine. *Washington*. Danbury, CT: Children's Press, 2003.

BOOKS ABOUT PLACES AND PEOPLE

Goodman, Michael E. *The History of the Seattle Mariners*. Mankato, MN: Creative Education, 2002.

Weintraub, Aileen. *How to Draw Washington State's Sights and Symbols*. New York: PowerKids Press, 2002.

DVDS AND VIDEOS

Hatzoff Productions. *Washington State's San Juan Islands*, 2005.

———. *Washington State: A Scenic Tour*, 2004.

———. *Washington State's Emerald City: Seattle*, 2002.

Access Washington

www.access.wa.gov/statefacts/index.aspx

The State Facts page of the official Washington State Web site has information about Washington's history, geography, state symbols, and more, as well as a state trivia game.

Washington State History Museum

www.washingtonhistory.org

The Washington State Historical Society's site offers links to online exhibits and a virtual tour of the museum. The site includes many articles from *Columbia* magazine, published by the society.

American Indians of the Pacific Northwest

http://content.lib.washington.edu/aipnw

American Indians of the Pacific Northwest, maintained by the University of Washington Libraries, is a collection of photographs, documents, and writings by historians and teachers about the Native Americans of Washington.

Experience Washington

www.experiencewashington.com

The state's tourism site has many maps and photographs of Washington, along with information about attractions and events.

Washington State Magazine

www.washington-state-magazine.wsu.edu

Washington State Magazine, published by Washington State University, has online articles and a gallery of photographs of the state's natural beauty, historic heritage, and people.

Index

Page numbers in **boldface** are illustrations and charts.

ABOUT THE AUTHOR

Rebecca Stefoff is the author of numerous works on history and science. She lives in Portland, Oregon, right across the Columbia River from Washington, which she visits often.